AJAMU X

The Tate Photography Series is a celebration of international and British photography in the Tate collection and an introduction to some of the most significant photographers at work today. Previous sets of four in the series have explored the themes of Community and Solidarity, and Ecology and Environment.

Each book focuses on an individual photographer and features a specially selected sequence of photographs, an introduction by a Tate curator and a conversation with, or statement by, the artist. These collaborative books as dialogues between artists and experts aim to enrich our understanding of photography and its connection to everyday life, and collectively they move from city streets to seashores, across landscapes and subcultures, through identities and interiors, in a visual travelogue of our world today.

The theme for Series Three is Queer and Visible, bringing together four artists who use photography to unfold valuable insights into queer life. Each artist uniquely reflects upon societal constructs of sexuality and race, and responds to the experience of living in a predominantly white and heteronormative society.

To see and to make seen, to work in good faith, to produce artful storytelling and resonant images – these are the qualities we seek from good photography. The artist-photographer notices and captures, calls for a moment of our divided and hurried attention, and reveals connection and pattern, emotion and meaning. The work sets out to expand the possible and make hearts and minds more spacious.

Series Three

3:1   **LAURA AGUILAR**
3:2   **SUNIL GUPTA**
3:3   **LYLE ASHTON HARRIS**
3:4   **AJAMU X**

AJAMU X

Edited by
Hannah Marsh

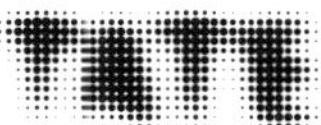

First published 2025 by order of the Tate Trustees
by Tate Publishing, a division of Tate Enterprises Ltd,
Millbank, London SW1P 4RG
www.tate.org.uk/publishing

A catalogue record for this book is available from
the British Library

ISBN 978 1 84976 956 3

Distributed in the United States and Canada
by ABRAMS, New York

Library of Congress Control Number applied for

Series Editor: Simon Armstrong
Senior Editor: Nicola Bion
Production: Bill Jones
Picture Research: Roz Hill
Designed by Sarah Boris
Colour reproduction by Westerham Press, London
Printed and bound in the UK by Westerham Press,
London

Front cover: *Yusuf* 2024
Back cover top: Black Circus Master series, 1997
Back cover bottom: from A Sensual Chorus of
Gestures, 2024

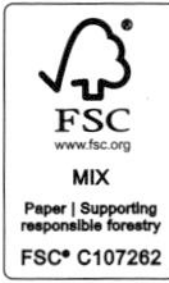

CONTENTS

INTRODUCTION

Darkroom/fine art photographic artist, activist and scholar Ajamu X was born in Huddersfield in 1963 and studied photography at Kitson College in Leeds. Alongside his practice, Ajamu founded the magazine *Black Liberation Activist Core* in 1985, and is the co-founder of 'rukus! Federation/Black LGBTQ Archive'. Production, making and process are at the centre of Ajamu's work, with his subject matter evoking a similar focus on sensuality. Most recently, Ajamu has explored the beauty and joy of the erotic. His imagery often challenges ideas associated with Black masculinity, gender and sexuality.

When studying in Leeds in 1987, Ajamu attended two talks he now regards as integral to his formation as an artist: a talk by David A. Bailey on Black photography, and the first National Black Gay Men's Conference. Shortly after this, Ajamu created his now iconic *Body Builder in Bra* photograph in 1990. Studiously considering lighting in a mode comparable to that of Renaissance painters, Ajamu tenderly sculpts the figure, accentuating his subject's back muscles through a thin lace bra that stretches and tears while protectively embracing the body. The work delicately unearths a moment of softness within a masculine space. The series was exhibited in the pivotal exhibition *Kiss My Genders* at the Hayward Gallery in 2019.

Describing himself as a 'craftsman', Ajamu's craft is divided into two moments, the first being the scene created within his studio, where his muses playfully perform his vision. The second entails the artist alone in the darkroom, carefully developing images guided by a deep understanding of the chemicals, each print bearing the artist's touch. *Feet of Duane Cyrus, Dancer* 1995 illustrates the sensual quality of Ajamu's process. Ajamu's attention to detail here is captivating – the foot evokes silk, the sea, a landscape. We are encouraged to consider the feeling of the print, and envision the entire dance the subject performs.

This work speaks of the artist's interest in Audre Lorde's text *Uses of the Erotic: The Erotic as Power*. Feet and hands are integral to the erotic for Ajamu, a source of fetish. Lorde states that if we are able to embrace and celebrate the erotic, all other strands of our lives are required to meet this same standard of joy.[1]

Furthermore, time is a precious medium within the process, enabling the artist to embody what is happening in the darkroom. Time is

1   Audre Lorde, Uses of the Erotic: The Erotic as Power, Virginia 1978.
2   Kevin Quashie, The Sovereignty of Quiet, New Jersey 2012.
3   Roland Barthes, Camera Lucida, new edn, London 1993, p.27.

halted, enabling meditation and reflection. The darkroom, where time and love are infused, becomes metaphorical of the internal self. One is afforded the opportunity to be quiet in the darkroom, a gift often denied in the outside world, especially in regard to Black communities and queer communities, who are – as discussed by philosopher Kevin Quashie – expected to be loud.[2]

'What is this thing called the photograph?'

The power of the photograph has long been explored in photographic history. Roland Barthes bestows great power upon the photograph in *Camera Lucida*, proposing the notion of 'punctum', photography's ability to 'wound' and 'prick' its viewer.[3] He relays feeling 'wounded' by the image of a Black American family dressed in their Sunday best attire, particularly the detail in a necklace worn by the mother. Barthes presumes the family are attempting to 'assume the white man's attributes', unaware of the self-fashioning and ingenuity integral to Black history and culture.[4]

The power of the photograph was first felt by Ajamu as a child, dressing up in Sunday best clothing, to pose for a photograph that would be sent home to family in Jamaica. The camera was thus understood by the artist from a young age as something with which one presented a certain version of oneself. Ajamu would eagerly await the return of the photo, wondering, 'what is this thing called the photograph?' It encapsulated a certain magic.

In Ajamu's early work the artist plays with his own identity under the lens of a camera, particularly his Self-Portrait in Wedding Dress series from 1993. Considering the symbolism of the wedding dress in Western culture, Ajamu interrogates identity through an alter ego, dispelling gender norms. Ajamu performs for the camera in 'best' clothing once again here, but importantly redefines it.

Camera Lucida was a book gifted to Ajamu by a professor who foresaw the artist's future as a photographic artist. As noted, Barthes speaks of the photograph's ability to 'prick' its viewer. Perhaps what Ajamu's photography does then, is *push* its viewer, to imaginatively consider what is held in the image beyond the visual.

Hannah Marsh
Assistant Curator, Contemporary British Art, Tate Britain

4   Audre Lorde, Uses of the Erotic: The Erotic as Power, Virginia 1978.
5   All quotes from Ajamu X are taken from a conversation between the artist and curator Hannah Marsh, 24 June 2024.

AJAMU X AND HANNAH MARSH IN CONVERSATION

Hannah Marsh: What initiated your interest in art? Do you have a specific memory of this?

Ajamu X: I was always drawn to be creative in some shape or form, but my idea of an artist was someone that painted or drew. And of course, I couldn't draw or paint, so photography was a way of being this idea of the artist through the camera. My mum bought me my first camera. It came from the catalogue Empire Stores, costing about £2.50 a week, and it was a Pentax K1000, which is a pocket camera and super lightweight. I used this camera to take images for the *Black Magazine* around 1985. I remember its metallic feeling and the shutter being extremely loud. It was a minimalist camera, so perfect for someone like me who wanted to learn about this medium.

HM   And you then went on to study photography in Leeds. How did this shape your practice?

AX   When I left school I went into catering, painting and decorating, but I would cover my bedroom in white sheets, get this big household lamp and then just shoot images of guys, self-portraits, images of life. I just played around within my bedroom-slash-studio and then a few years later I went to Leeds Kitson College to study photography, printing and design. We looked at the work of Ansel Adams and Irving Penn – whose work I loved then and still love now – but I was looking for Black photographers, and gay photographers. Then there was a talk on Black photography by photographer and academic David A. Bailey in 1987 organised by artist Maud Sulter, and I was also introduced to the work of Rotimi Fani-Kayode, so I was able to bring race and sexuality into the same frame. The head of department said, 'I think you should actually leave the course and follow this thing called photography'. He gave me two books as presents. One was *Black Skin, White Masks* by Frantz Fanon, and the other *Camera Lucida* by Roland Barthes. I was not sure what to make of his comment at the time but years on it made a lot of sense.

HM   So much of your practice consists of you photographing other people, your muses, collaborators, friends, but of course you've worked a lot in self-portraiture too. Can you expand on the space that photography enables for an exploration of the self?

AX   Self-portraiture for me is key because in the early years I couldn't find the models, but of course I always had access to myself. Early in my practice my home space was also my studio. If an idea came up at two o'clock in the morning I could just go upstairs and play around in portrait, so naturally it's going to be the most accessible thing that I have. Self-portraiture then is a way to interrogate not just who I am in terms of my identity and sexuality, but more importantly, who I can fantasise myself to be. I've always had, over the years, various alter egos that I've played around with. There are the S&M kink images, and Master Aaab is another character. Master Aaab is taken from one of my role models, Dirg Aaab-Richards, a queer activist who's not into kink, I need to say that publicly, but I find it funny that I've taken his name. Key for portraits is playfulness, so I like seeing what then happens if I play around with the wedding dress, knowing what the wedding dress signifies in Western culture.

And then also some of my self-portraits are based on particular sexual experiences that I've had, so they are in-jokes. I do like the idea of playing around with one's identity. I'm not necessarily drawn to discovery, but I'm drawn to invention. Yeah, I find that more exciting.

HM   Wonderful. And that perfectly brings me to the influence of Bell Hooks upon your practice. Hooks asks, how do we move beyond just critiquing the status quo? How can we transform the image, creating alternative ways of looking? Your work performs this notion of transformation through its inventive quality, dispelling rigid ideas around identity.

AX   It's all about pushing against the trap of identity thinking and representation. I'm not saying that those things don't have a place – they do – but I think that there is a danger of only looking through the lens of Black and queer experience. The obsession with identity thinking and representation can mean people sidestep or dismiss process and production, which is a major part of the photography act. I also want my work to be spoken about within the history of photography more widely. Of course, the history of photography has problematised race and sexuality, but it's about asking how to inhabit that tension, how does my work speak to that history, where is its departure?

And yes, in terms of transforming the image, what happens when we ask questions around pleasures, eroticism and joy – the joy and pleasure in the act of making this thing called the photograph? A lot of my work is around Black queer bodies and intimacy is key, but it's also about how I am intimate with the process, and what I am working with as a photographer. I touch those chemicals and they touch me.

HM   The relationship between the materiality of the body and the material process in your work is extraordinary, you feel so present in each print. Audre Lorde's text *The Erotic as Power* underpins this approach to making. Could you elaborate on this?

AX   Ah yes, *The Erotic as Power*, my manifesto! I think what that text does, for me, is highlight joy. Historically, lots of our Black and queer activism work has ignored the erotic, ignored joy, to focus on the political. But also there is a reluctance to talk about it just for itself too – pleasure for pleasure's sake, without terminology like 'refusal' and 'resistance' coming into the conversation. And I think there is a reluctance to talk about the actual material body itself, and the materiality of the things that we work with as Black and brown queer artists, as well.

HM: That relationship between the body and the process is really apparent in how you consider the darkroom too.

AX   The darkroom is a place for contemplation and reflection, working things through – it's a temporal space, something that I enjoy for x amount of hours. And there's something about being able to shut the world out for a while. It's just me and the print, me and the chemical, me and the red light, me and water running, so then once again, I can embody what's happening in there. What happens in there is not representable but is sensed or felt naturally. Part of the beauty of the process is that we also don't always know what our process is. The darkroom has a sense of aura – it's mythical so you escape for a while. The darkroom allows you to be more in tune with your body, its movement, its gestures.

HM   It's amazing to hear you describe your body being part of the process, your hand touching and manipulating the chemicals and the water, the movement and gestures, the precision and detail – it sounds very painterly! Which is interesting in relation to your childhood understanding of the artist as someone who paints.

AX Yes! And that's the reason I've been drawn to the platinum print. It hovers between the painterly and the photographic. There is something as well in the body being a darkroom, you become aware of its movement, its rhythm, its rituals. And then also, as I said before, part of the process is unknowable. There's always an element of chance, and risk. That's why I love talking about production process more, so people can get a sense of what's going on.

HM The installation of the darkroom in your show at Autograph in 2023 was incredible. There was something in the materiality of it too that felt like the interior of a body, which chimes with what you have just beautifully described.

AX Yes, and I think photography privileges the visual, but in the darkroom the other senses kick in: the sonic, the tactility, the smell is important too. I think, for me, we make sense of the world, not only through the privilege of visual eye, but through all the senses. The darkroom is a space that brings it all together.

Lots of the early conversations around photography, via Barthes, semiotics via Marx, and 1980s and 1990s theory around photography was about how we think about the photograph. I'm more concerned with how we feel this thing called the photograph. I do not believe that we only encounter the image through the visual – we sense there are other things going on.

That's where the lighting has got to do something, the placing has got to do something, the composition has got to do something, all of everything in the frame has got to do something –just trying to give people a sense of what is outside the frame.

HM Allusions to what is happening outside the frame are very pertinent in your body of work in the exhibition *A Sensual Chorus of Gestures* at Amanda Wilkinson Gallery (2024) where hands almost become a way of seeing, and the relationship between gestures and sight too is explored.

AX I do like the idea of hands being able to see – hands are central to the darkroom process and the darkroom. So now I'm talking about both the photographic darkroom and the sex darkroom. When we look at

Renaissance paintings around, you know, Christ, the hands are not rigid. They're very graceful hands. So naturally, I've been trying to draw upon those, and those hands I've seen in classical painting. So it's kind of the gesture of the hand or the movement of the hand. For those of us who have had the pleasure of being in a sex darkroom, the light is lowered, so actually it's the hands that come in. A key component of the sexual encounter with people is through the hands.

I am also grappling with those things we cannot see, the gestures we make in certain moments. I am thinking about gestures when I'm making the platinum print too. The series I have made that captures the gestures people make in the moment of orgasm, is really thinking about the space the body enters in that moment, what I call 'elsewhere space'. If you look at, say, brothers and sisters in the Pentecostal Black church, in a moment of rapture, I am trying to capture that particular type of energy. And I think that for a lot of people who have then had that experience, something is put on hold for that nanosecond. Identity is lost, the sociological is lost. People go somewhere, something else is going on, for some it feels spiritual. When we see historical paintings of someone with their eyes closed we get a sense that they have entered somewhere else. So again, capturing that gesture in that moment is interesting. And there's something in allowing yourself to lose yourself in that moment.

HM The works we have just discussed expound clear ideas: around gestures, this in-between space, hands as sites to determine the world through. Is it often you have an idea before shooting, or can the shoots be more intuitive and spontaneous? How do your muses perform your vision?

AX Sometimes I might have an idea before the shoot. The image with the crow and the eggs, for example, just came to me one night in bed when I couldn't sleep. First thing next morning I went online to buy some wings, and then went to the market to buy some eggs. I called a friend of mine and said I've got an idea, and we started shooting. I keep a notebook by my bed so I can always sketch things that come to me.

And then with my muses sometimes it's just about playing around with ideas and seeing where it goes. In the process of playing, an amazing image is produced. Objects I love always appear too, like heels, so I will have certain objects ready in the space. And then sometimes the muse gives me what I call a 'gift image'. The gift image could just be a gesture that they will do naturally, and I am like 'wow, that's the image'. I remember being told by a photographer about thirty years ago, if you have an idea, push it to its extreme and you'll find something in that process of pushing. My muses understand me, they allow me to play around, and are generally very close friends, lovers, ex-lovers or fuck buddies. Also, I suppose I tap into sexual experiences I know my friends have had, a nod to that, or a nod to things that turn me on or sexual encounters I have had.

HM   So there is something about the space being very comfortable for you all, that then allows for your vision to develop. The muses are artists in their own right too, in how they move and perform.

AX   Exactly, and my models know that the body is a conduit I am working through. It's not about them. There is a concept they are helping me to realise. Yeah. Music is key too – I always come back to certain kind of albums. Music always brings a certain kind of energy to the shoots.

There's a quote by Ansel Adams, my favourite quote, and he basically says that you don't take a picture with the camera. You take a picture with all the images you have seen, all the books you've read, all the music you've heard, and all the people that you've loved. I find that that, for me, is what is happening when I take pictures – everything is part of my process.

HM   Wow, yes, so your own experiences frame the image, that's a wonderful notion.

AX   British humour plays a big role in influencing my work too. I do say to people, if you were born and raised in this country in the 1960s and 1970s, you grew up on *Carry On* movies. British humour always has this double entendre going on, so that happens as well in my work, that playfulness. That means that the image can be read in multiple ways. And I think that for a photograph to work, it's got to be read in multiple ways. And then that also means you can't always pin down the photographer on exactly what they were thinking. And then of course there's Jamaican humour, African humour – all of that informs how I think.

Also, I'm a northerner, I'm not just British. As a northerner we talk quite frankly and openly, and the work draws upon that open energy, like, yes this work is about two guys fucking. There is a northern saying, 'chocolate is chocolate, it's not confectionery', so I don't dress things up.

HM   Brilliant, and yes, there is a certain directness in your work, perhaps one of the reasons why it is so visually arresting, along with its beauty and detail. To conclude, what are you working towards or thinking about currently?

AX   My next body of work is going to be a book project. I want to re-engage with *The Joy of Sex*. Those books were iconic on one level – they came out of a particular historical moment. But within the book there are no Black bodies. There are no brown bodies. If you look at the lesbian *Joy of Sex* there are still no Black or brown bodies. And then in the gay *Joy of Sex*, there's still the absence of Black bodies.

HM   So you're thinking about that sense of absence?

AX   Yes, interrogating that absence, by speaking back to the text, creating a conversation around it through my own lens, and making photographs in response to it. I am also really interested in interrogating the images that were featured in some of the books, because for me, they were not sexy at all. So I am thinking about how I can re-write this to be more sexy. I am asking, where is the 'joy' in *The Joy of Sex*?

HM   Yes, unearth the joy! Sounds fantastic, I look forward to it and thank you so much, Ajamu.

AX   Thank you, it's been wonderful.

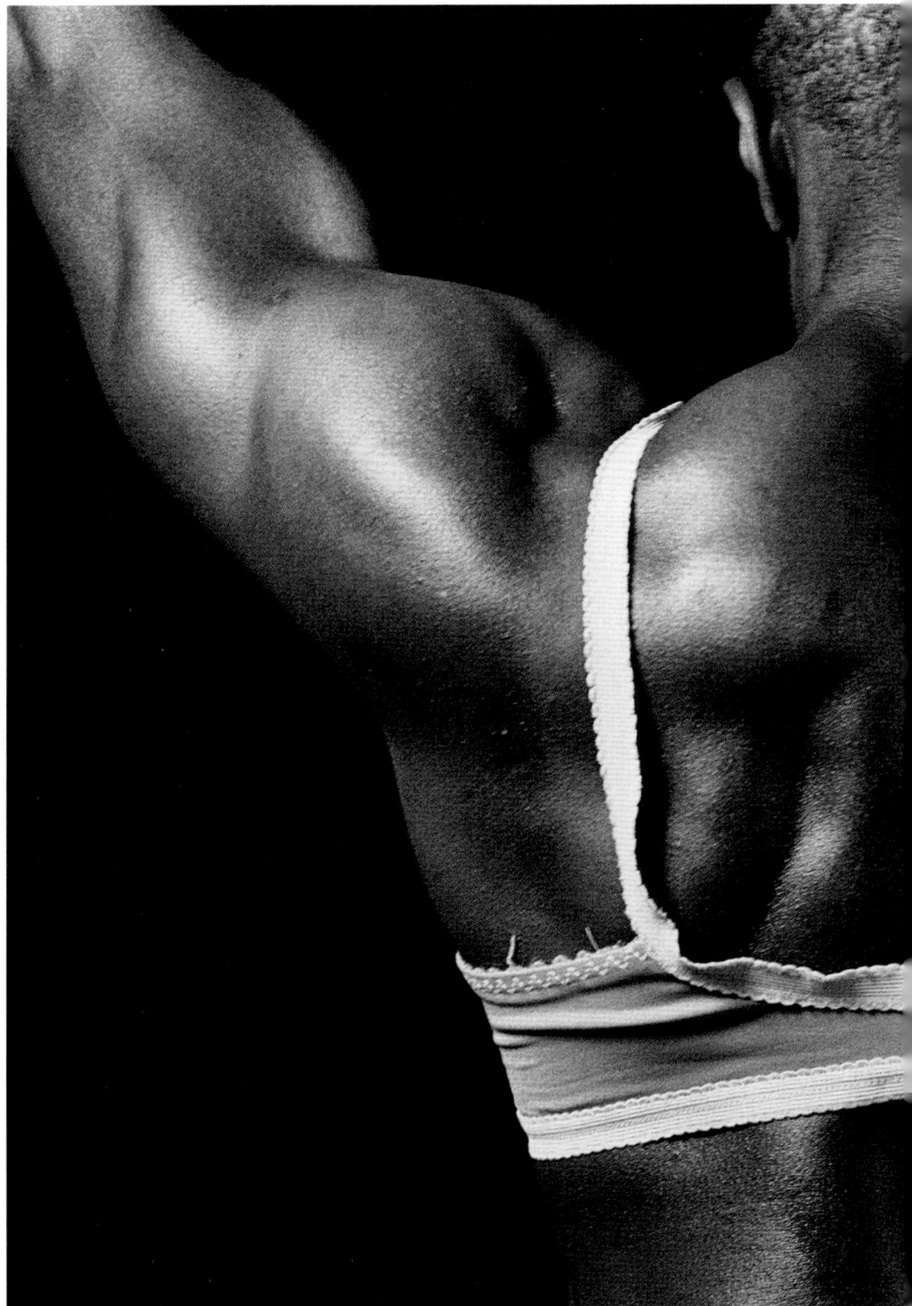

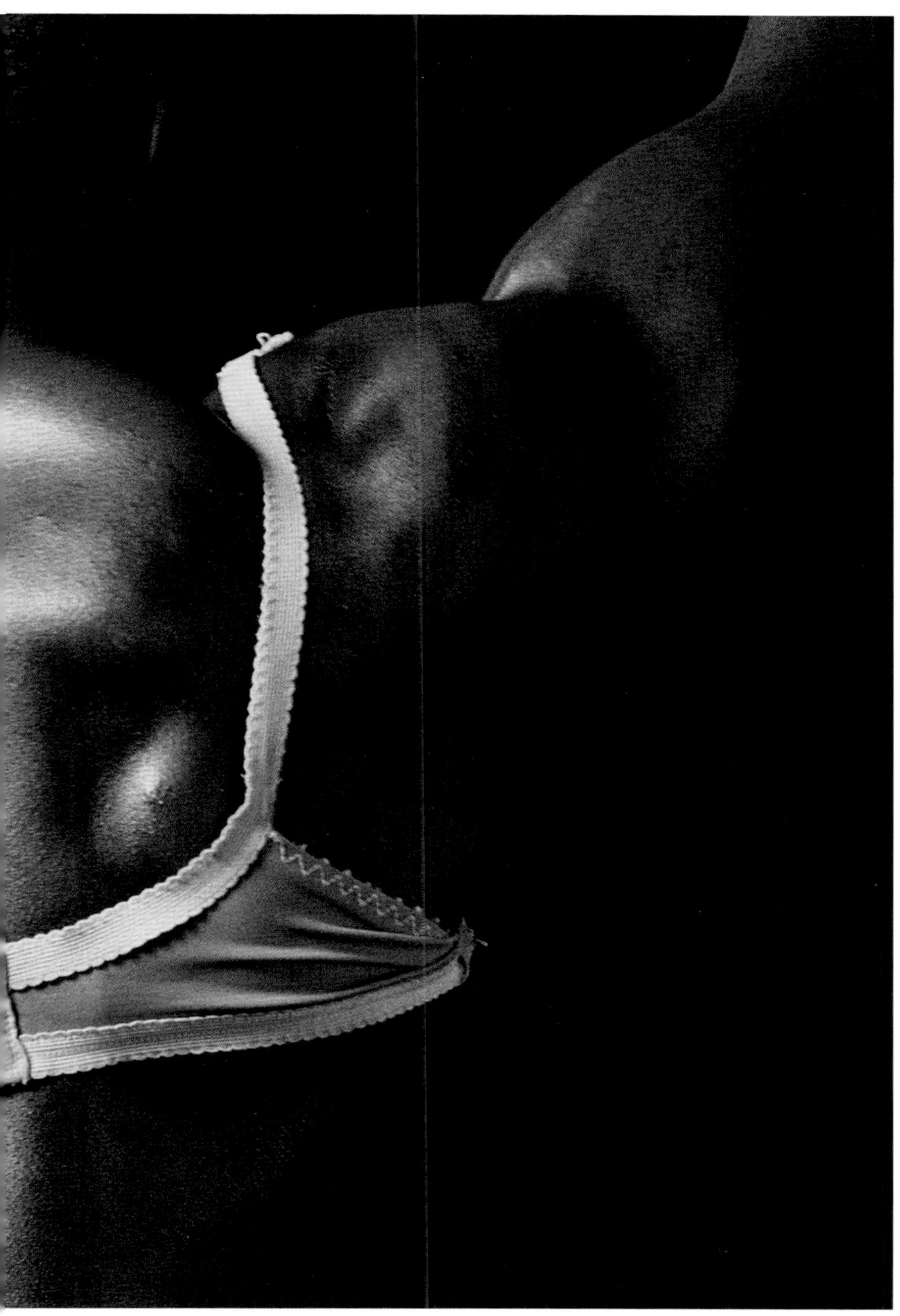

   Body Builder in Bra 1990

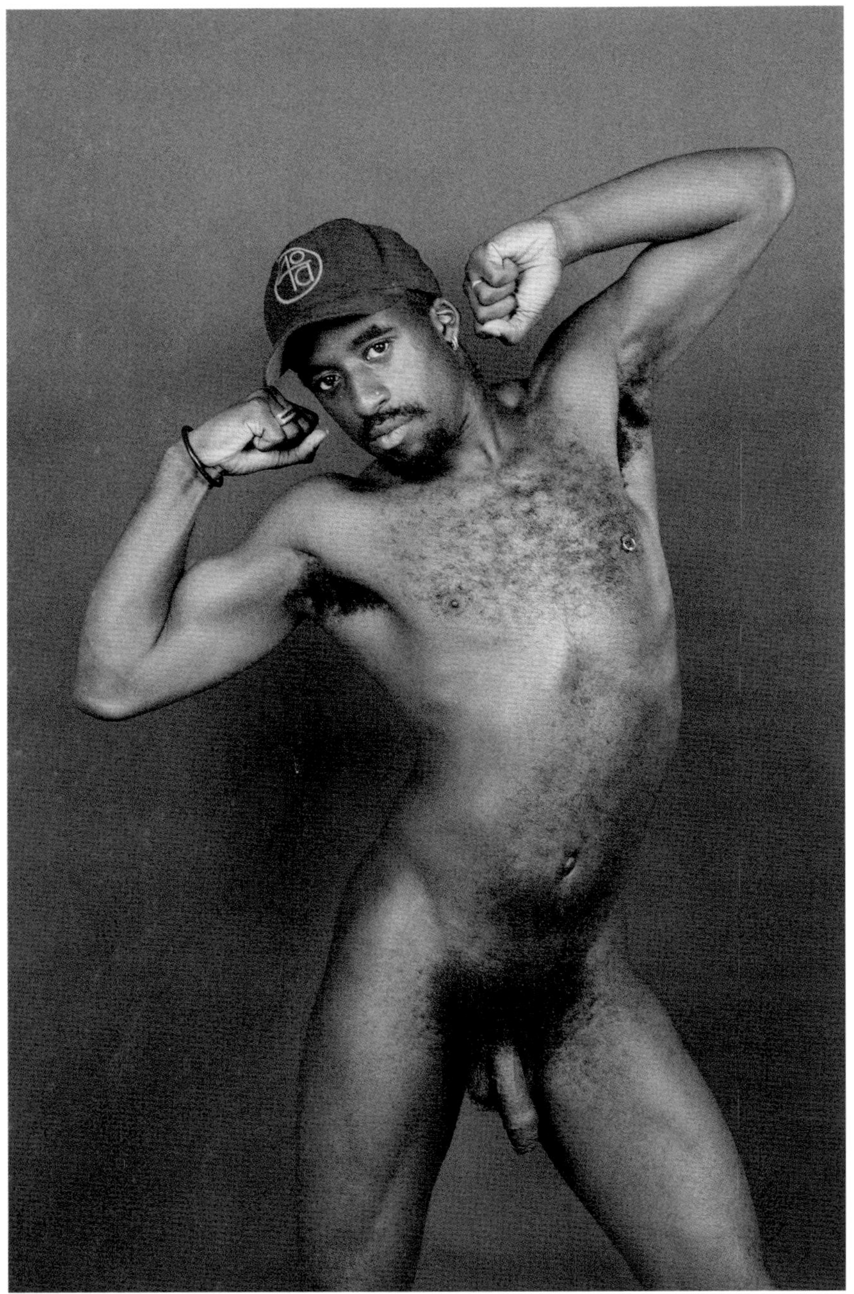

   Self Portrait [1] (Diamond Porn Star) 1992

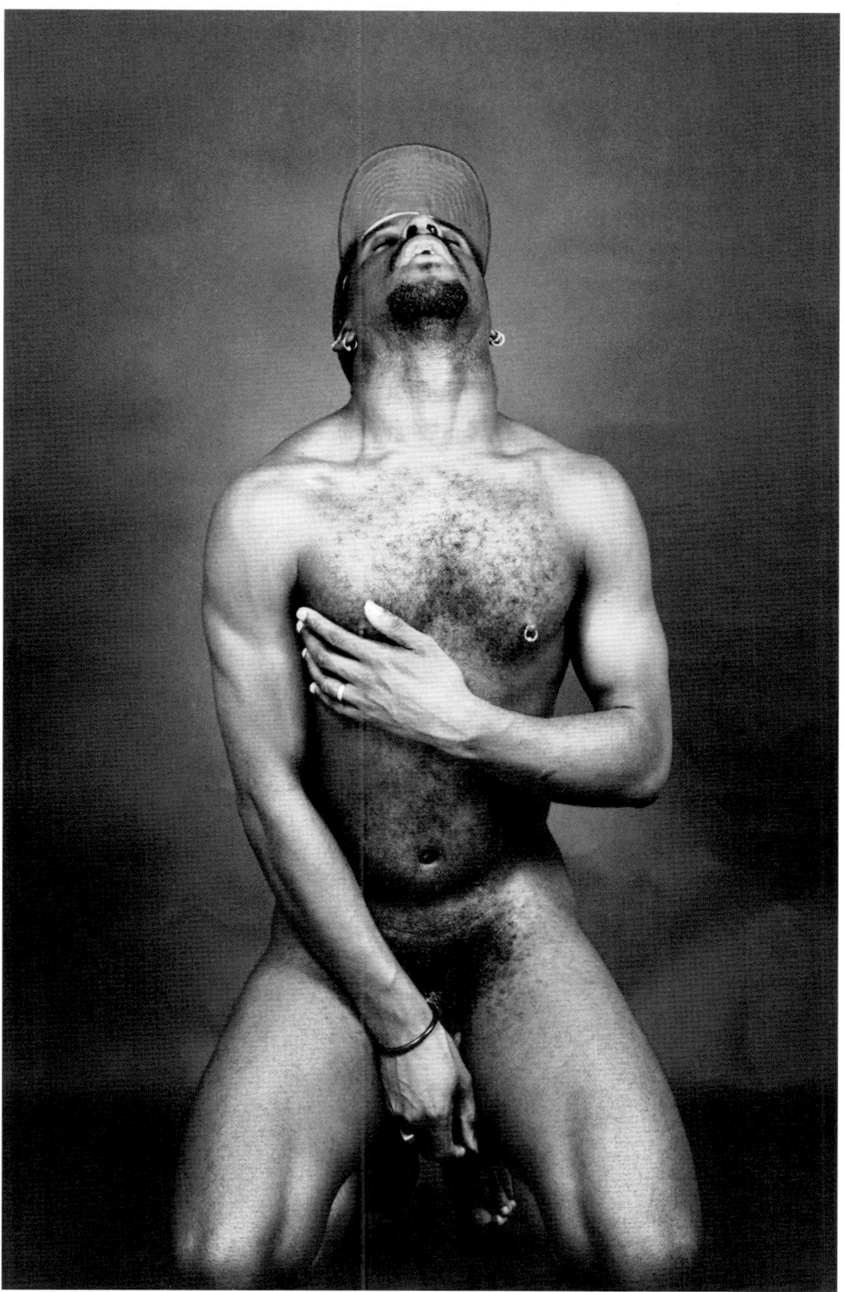

    Self Portrait [2] (Diamond Porn Star) 1992

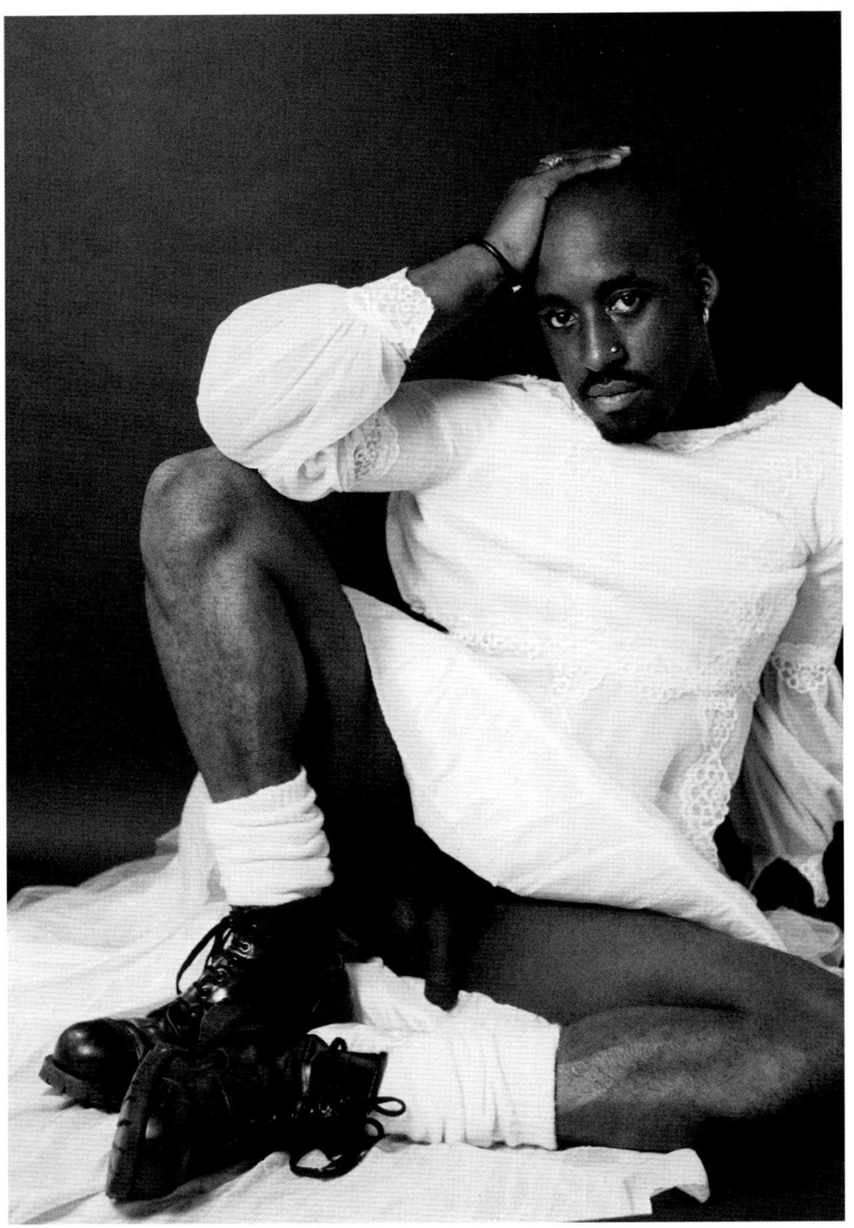

 Self-Portrait (Wedding Dress series) 1993

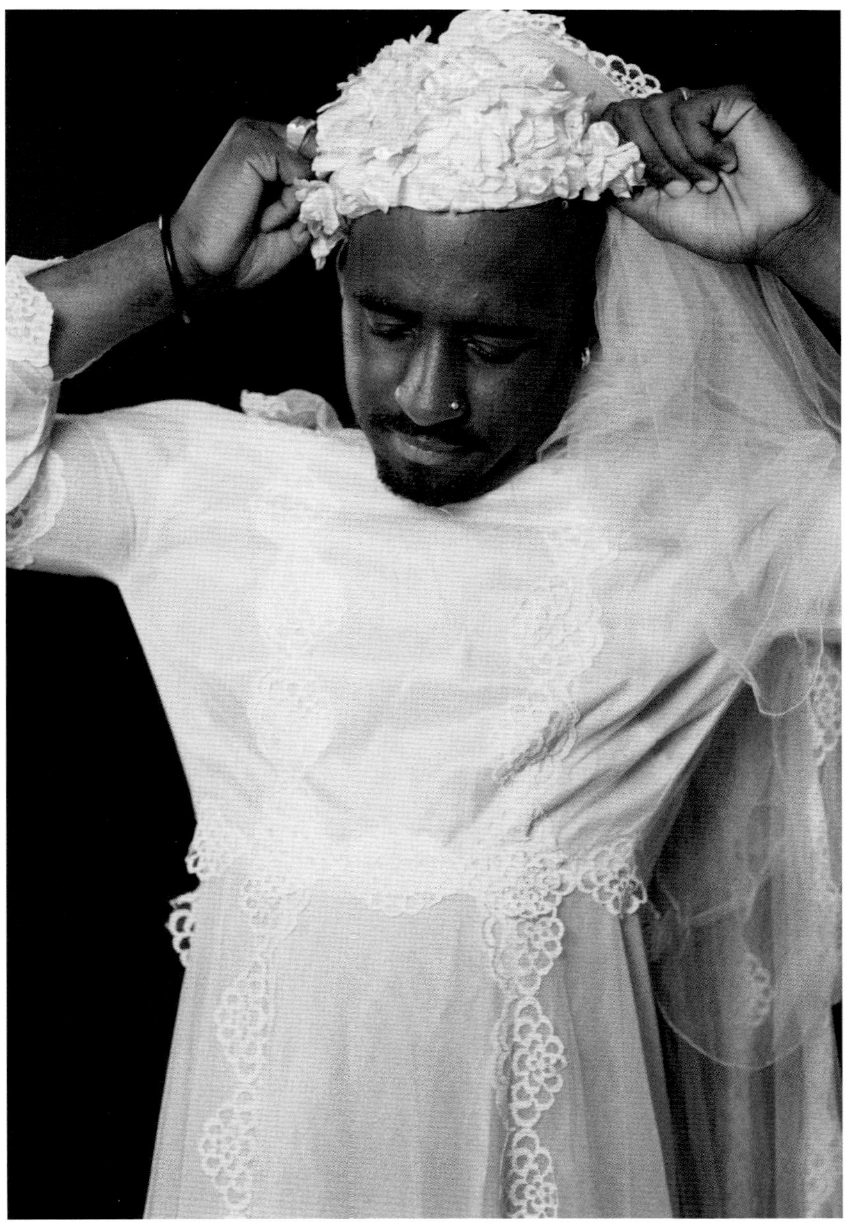

  Self-Portrait (Wedding Dress Series) 1992

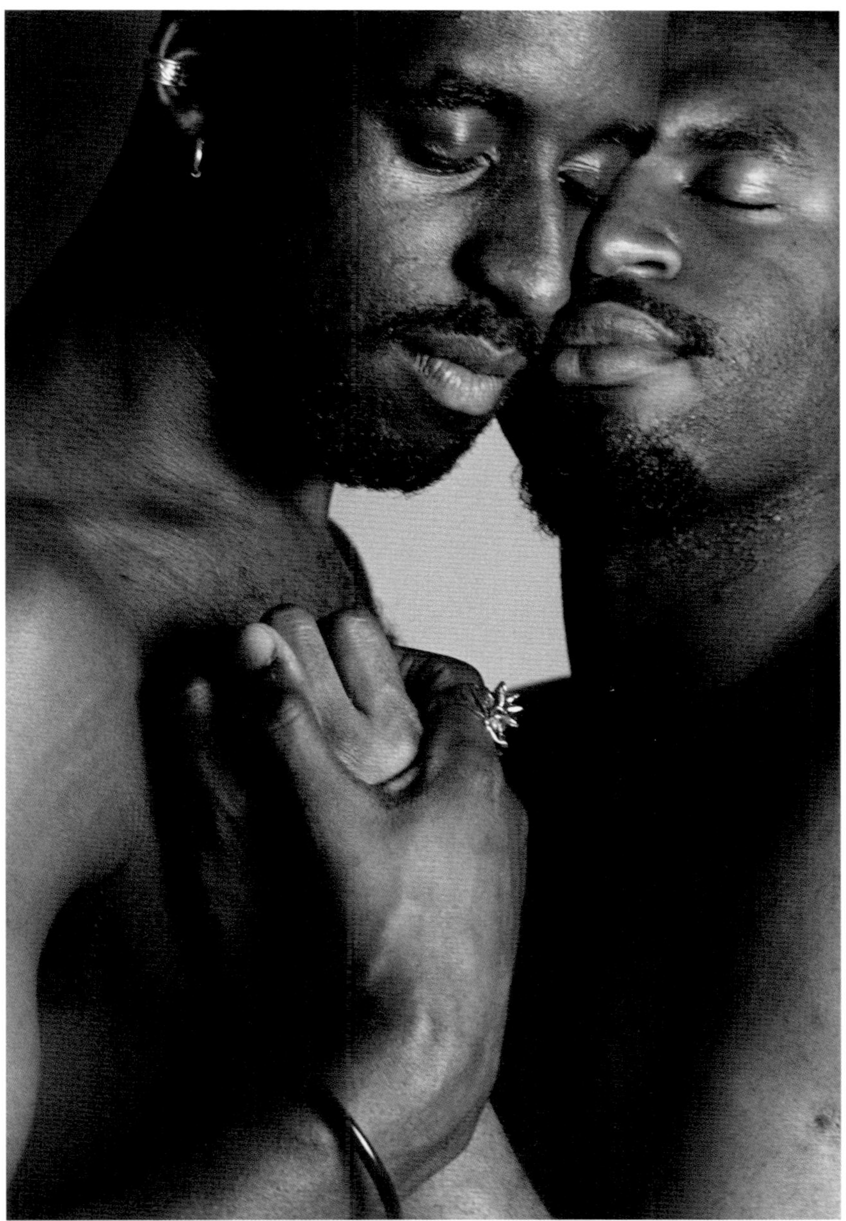

    Long Time Companion 1992

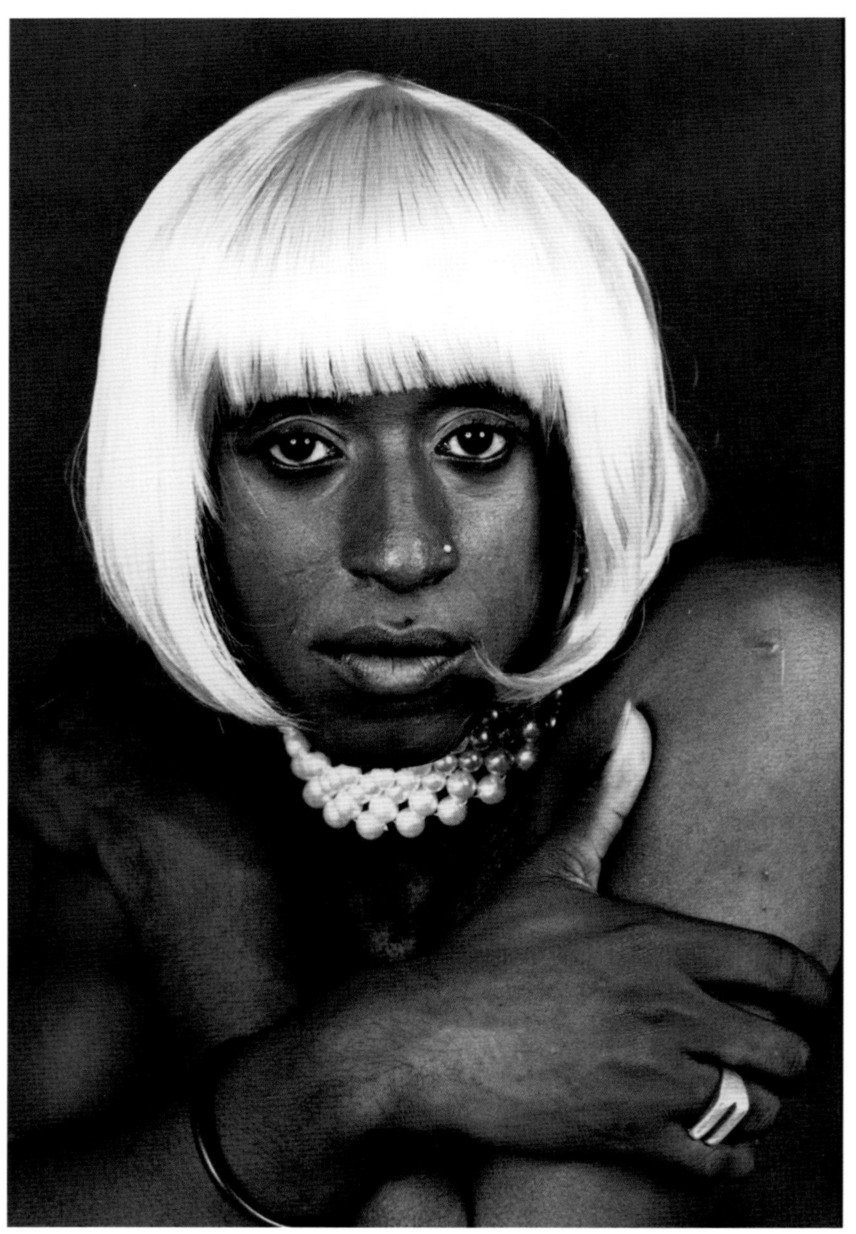

    Self-Portrait 1993

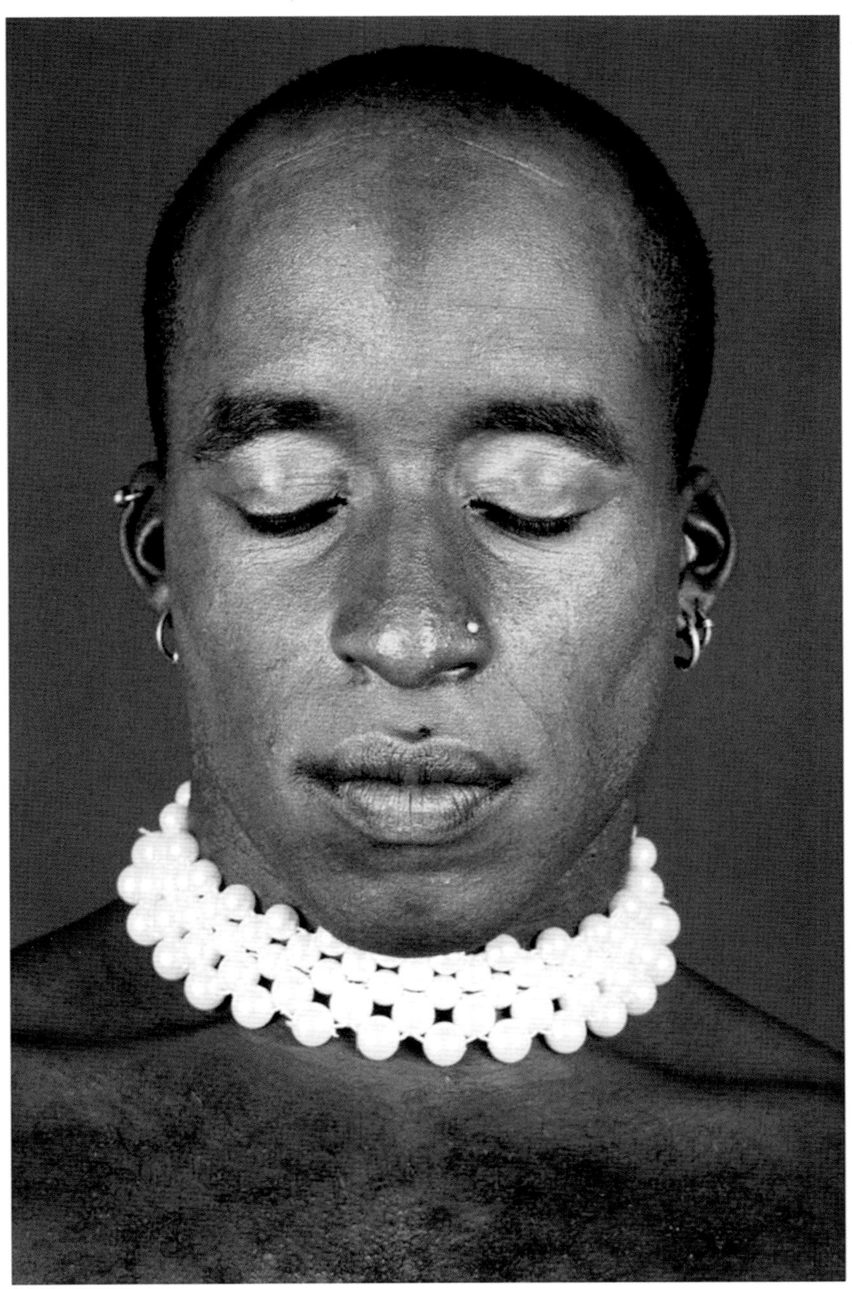

    Self -Portrait 1993

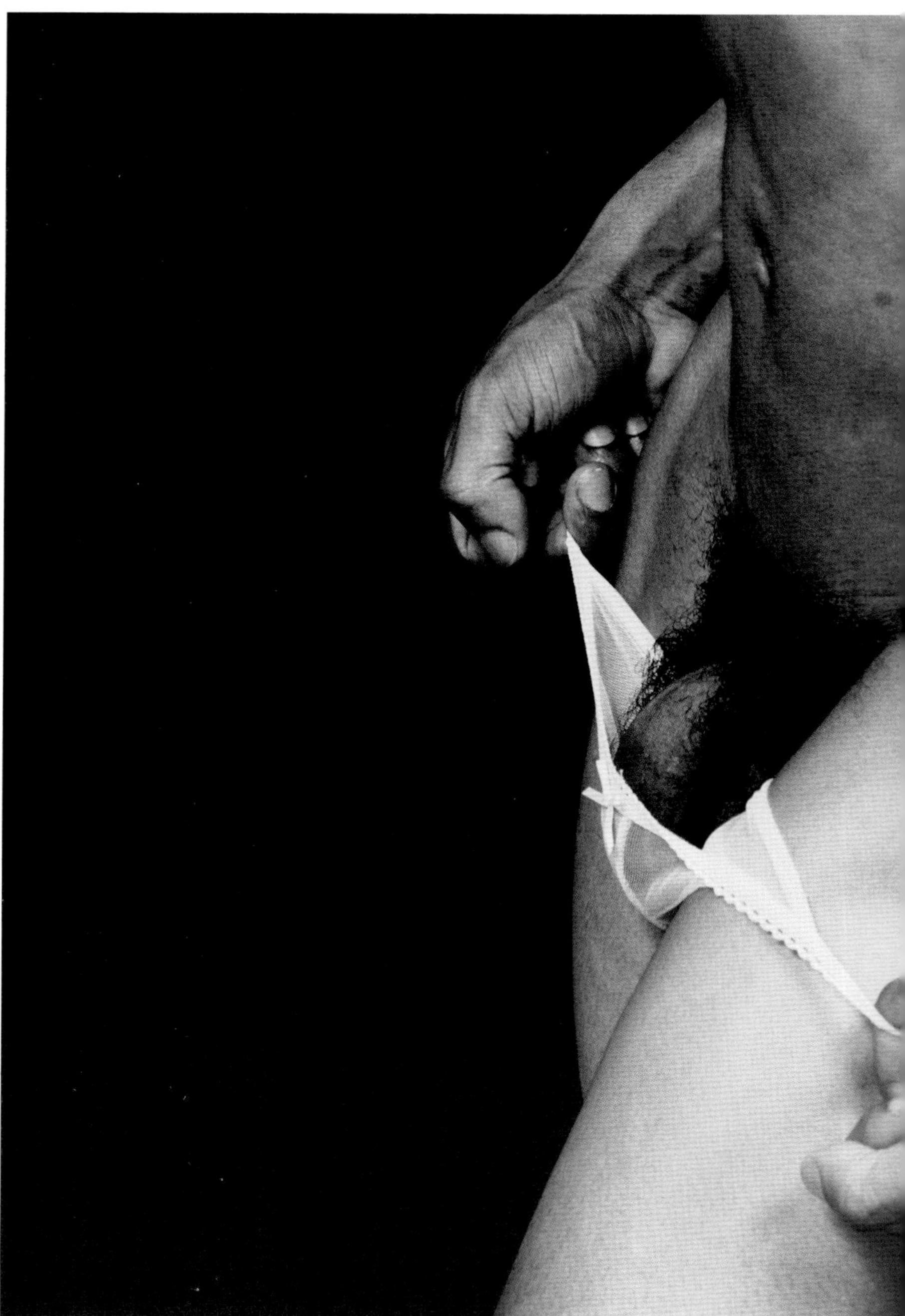

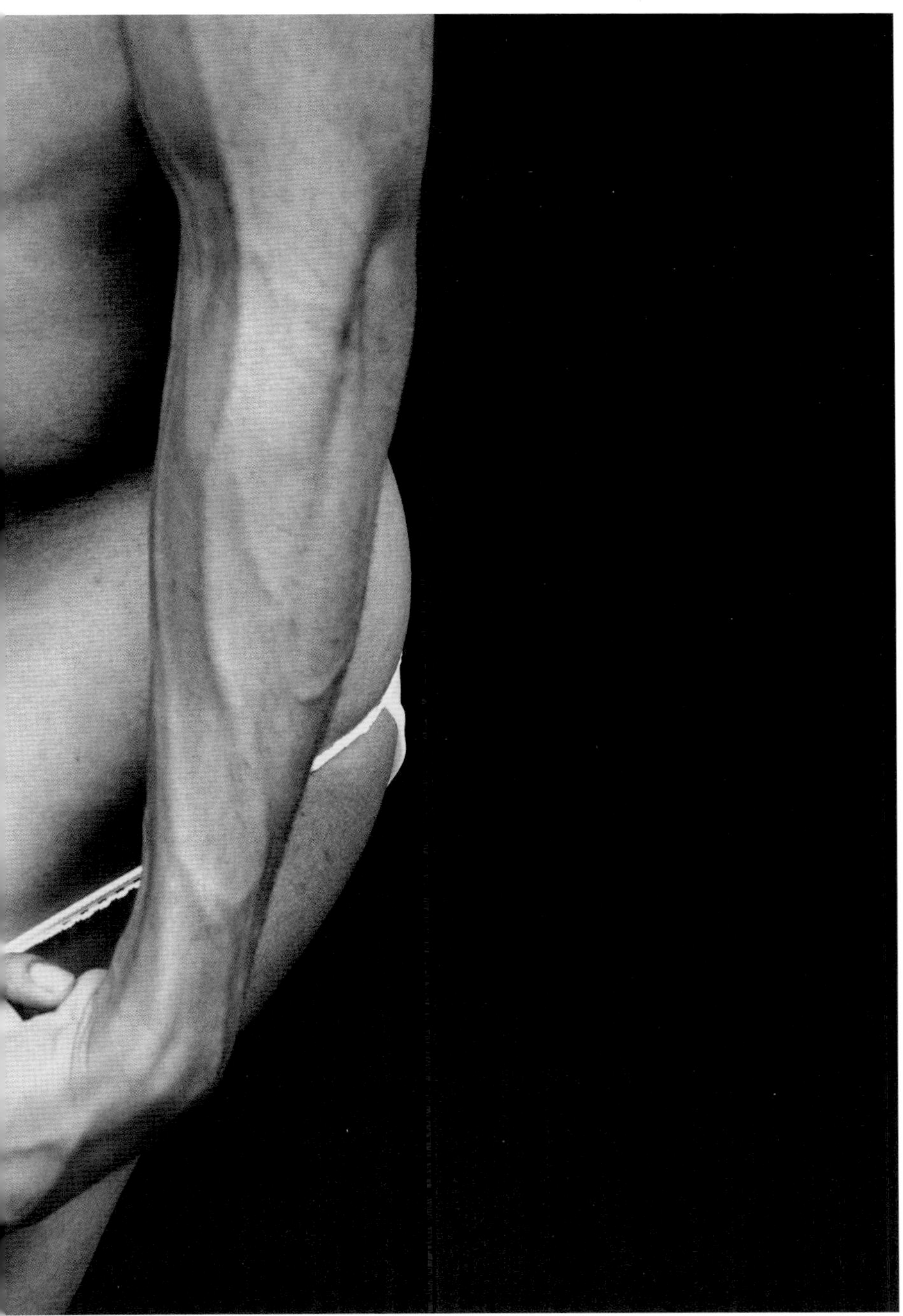

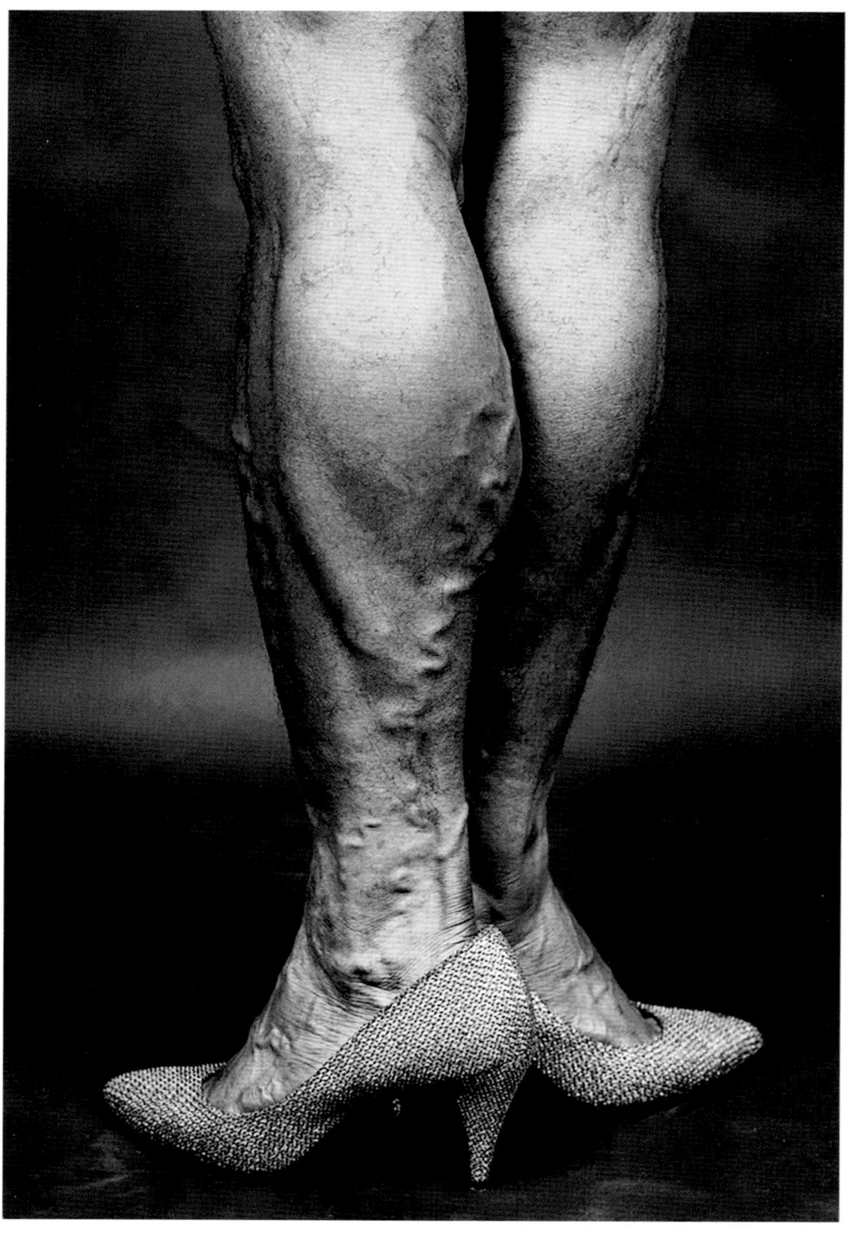

        Heels 1993

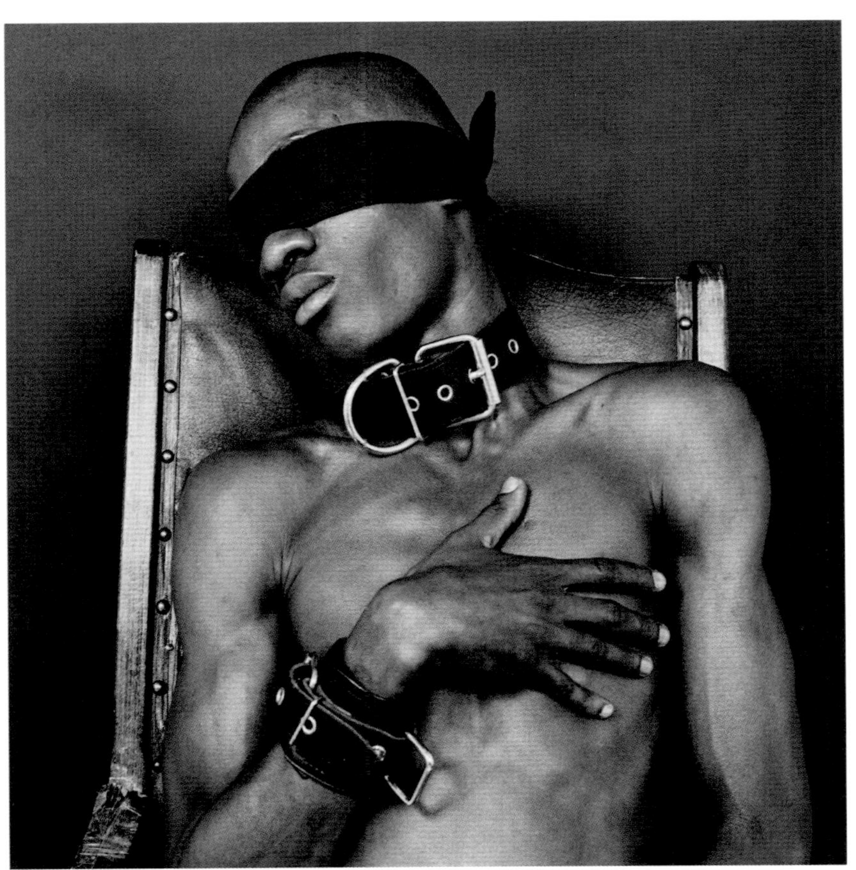

   Black Circus Master series, 1997

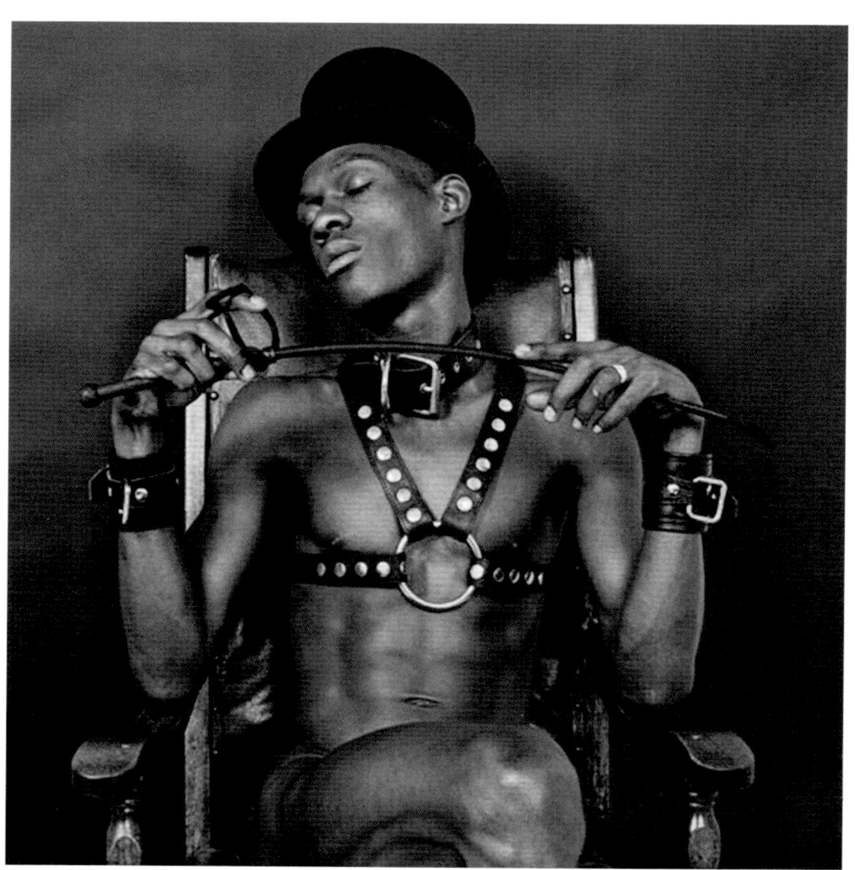

30   Black Circus Master series, 1997

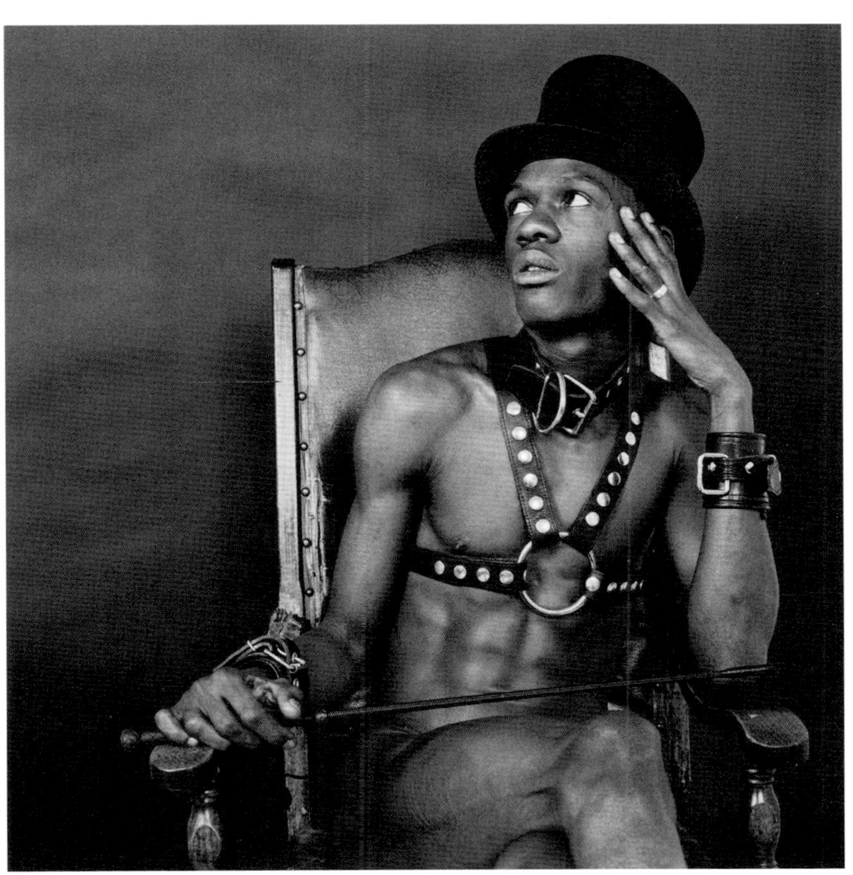

  Black Circus Master series, 1997

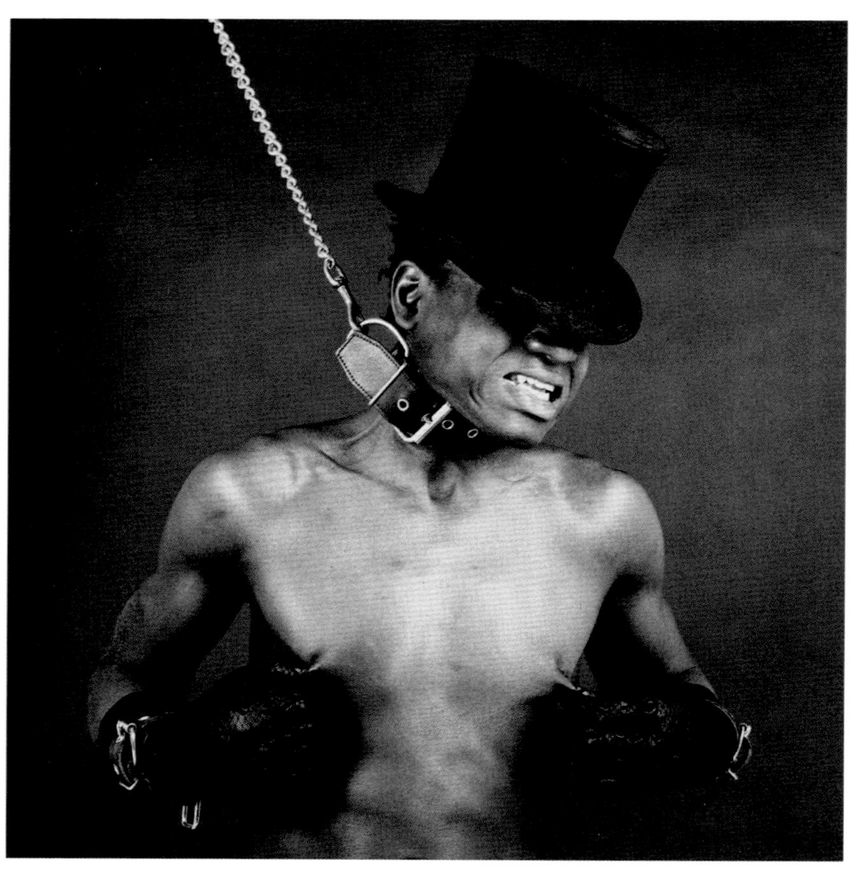

   Homage to Leopold van Sacher-Masoch 1998

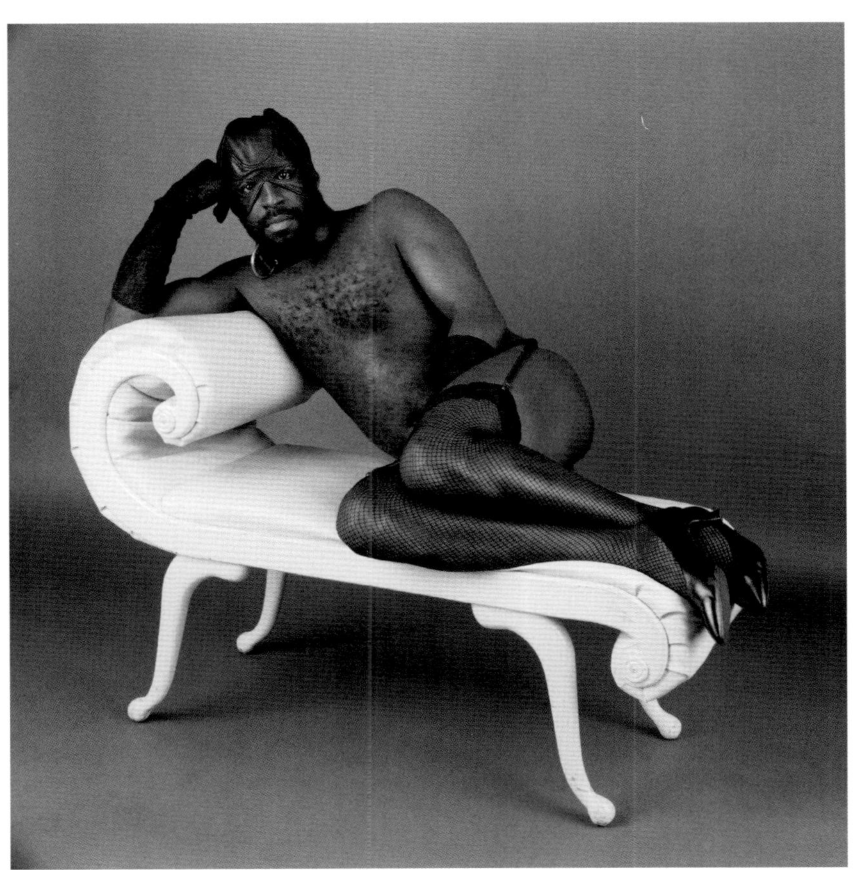

33   *Self-Portrait on Chez Lounge* 1998

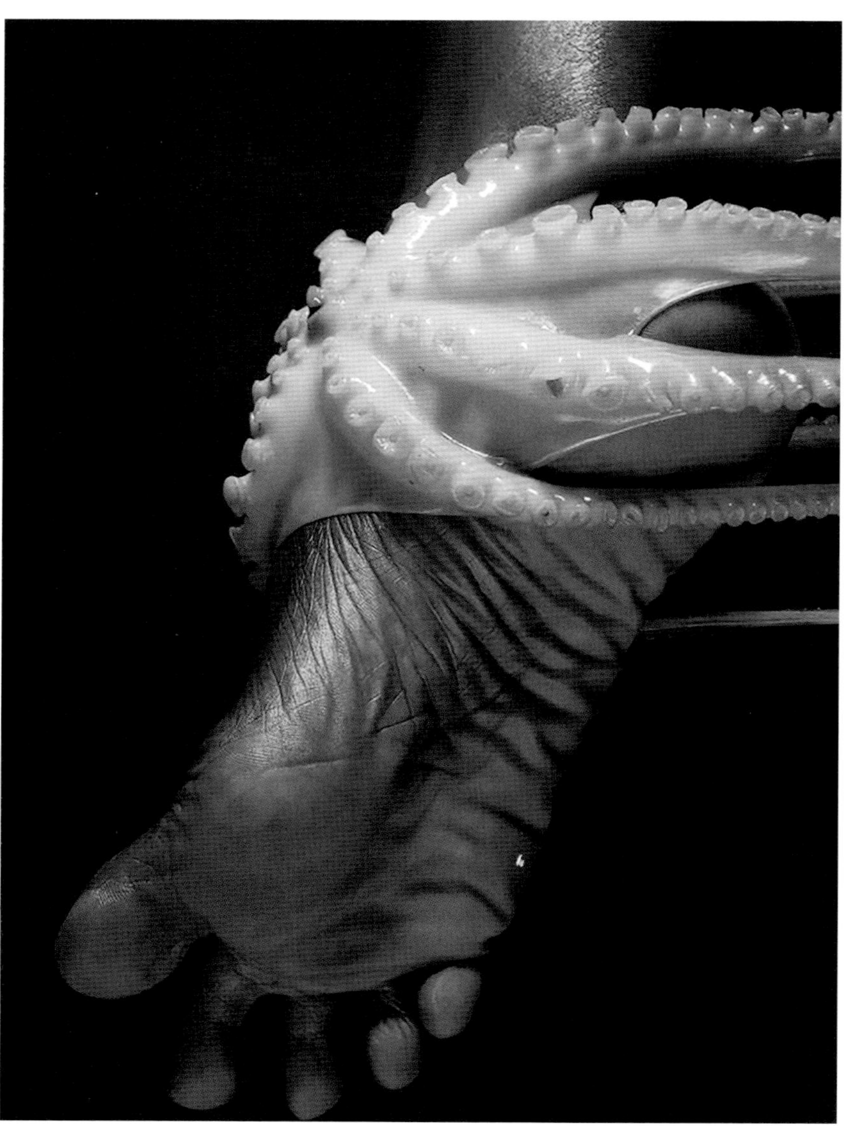

    Feet of Duane Cyrus 2015

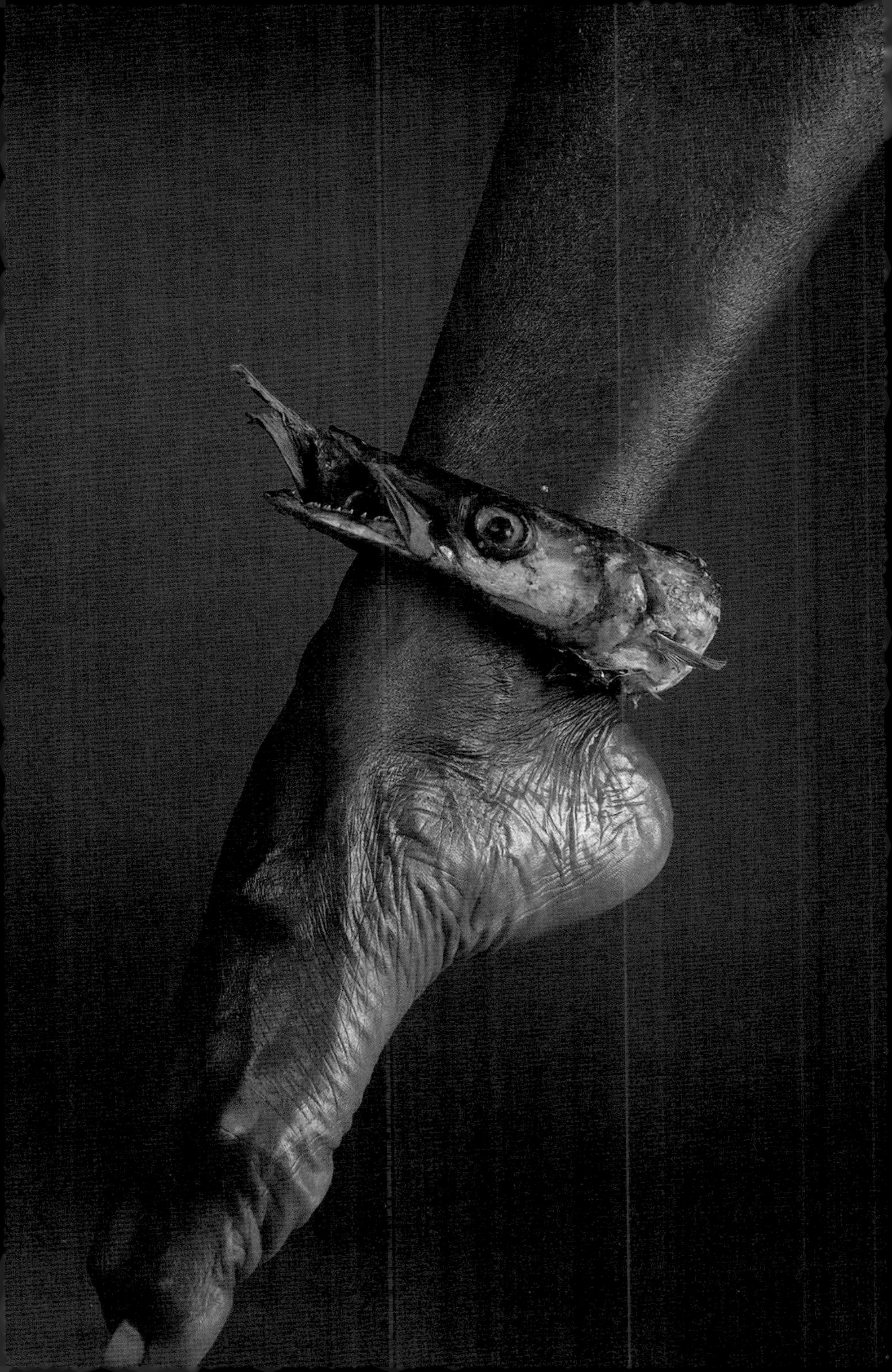

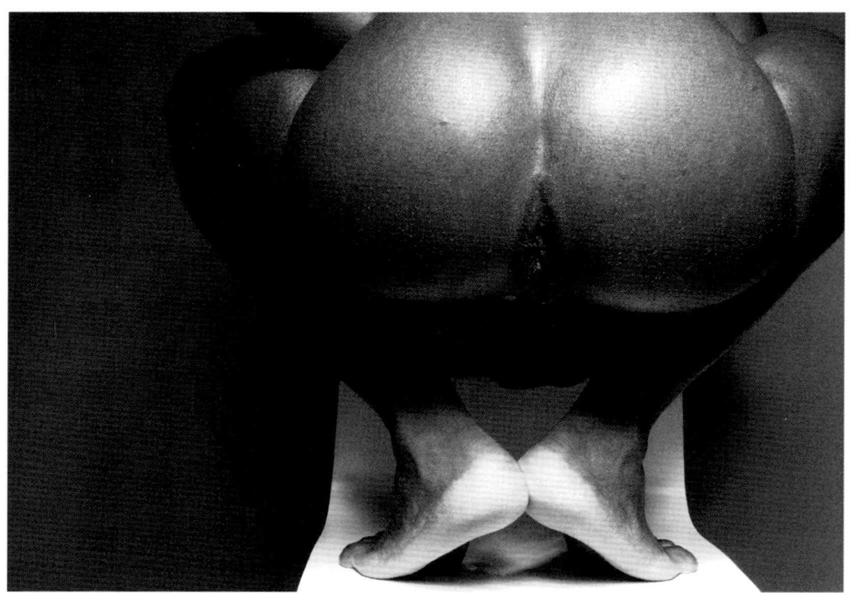

 White Feet (after Rotimi Fani-Kayode) 2015

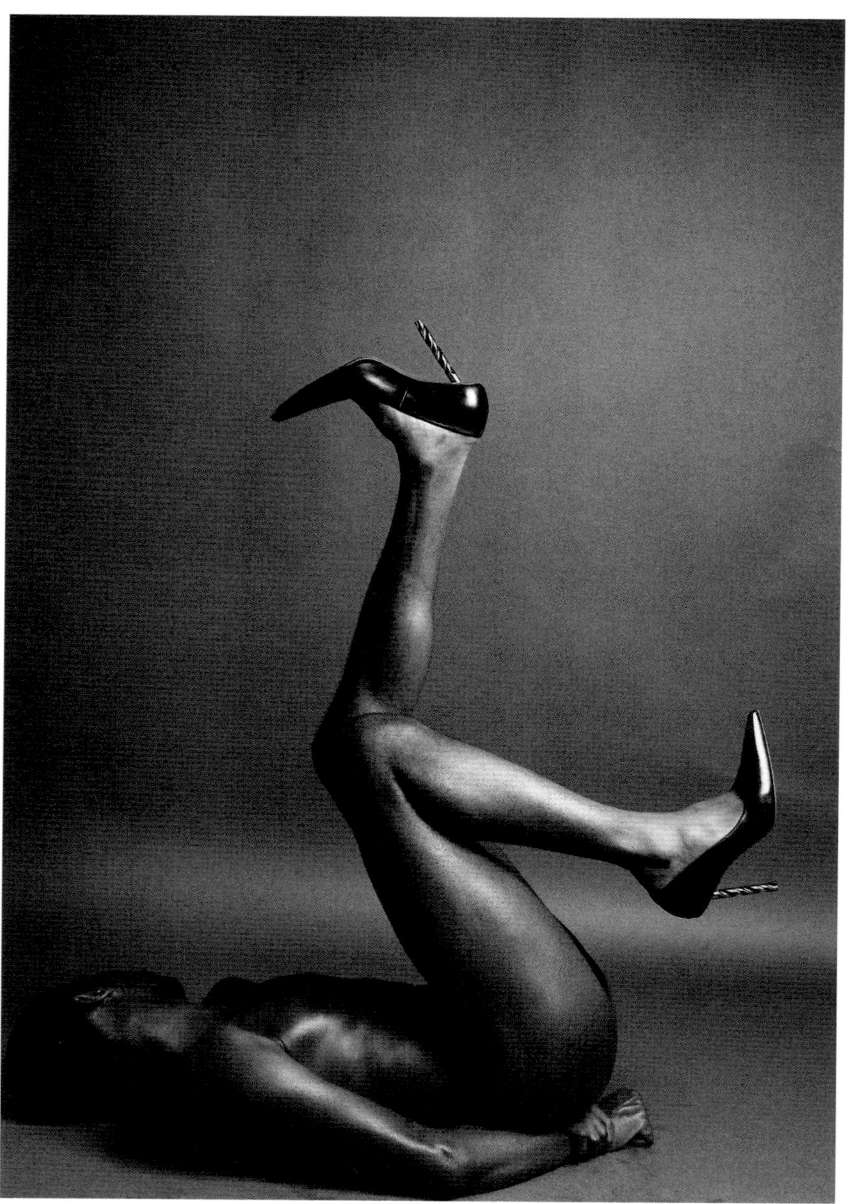

   Seyon Amosu, Muse 2020

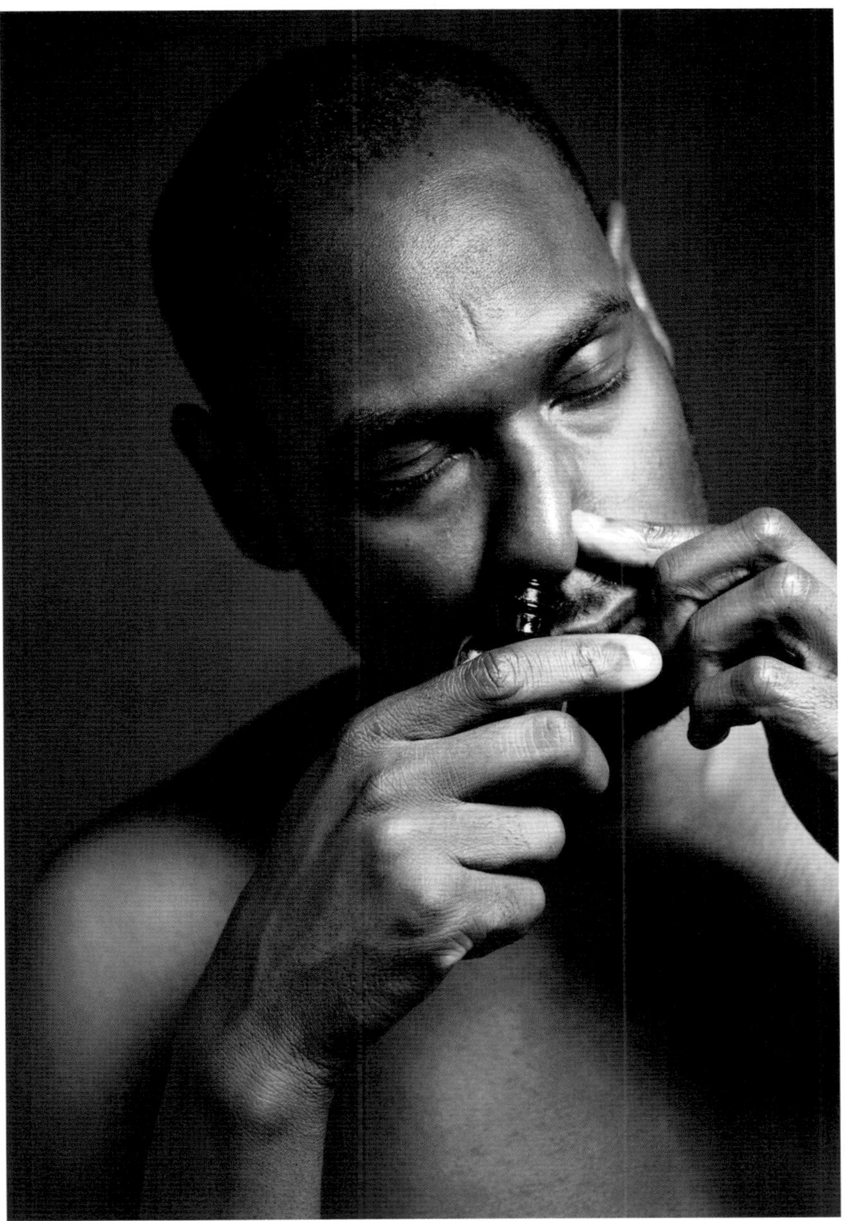

  Poppers (Amyl Nitrate) 2021

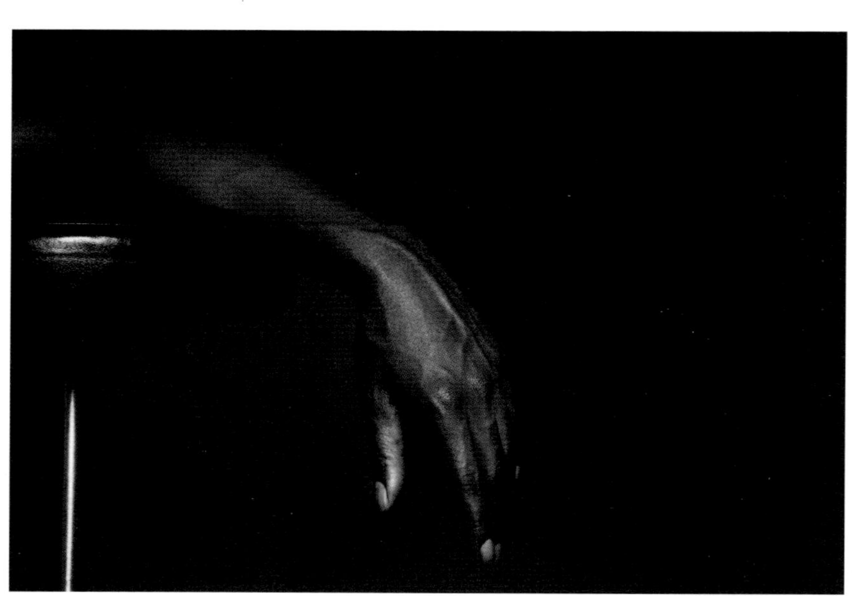

 PN 1916/63 - 1 2022, from the series Very Private

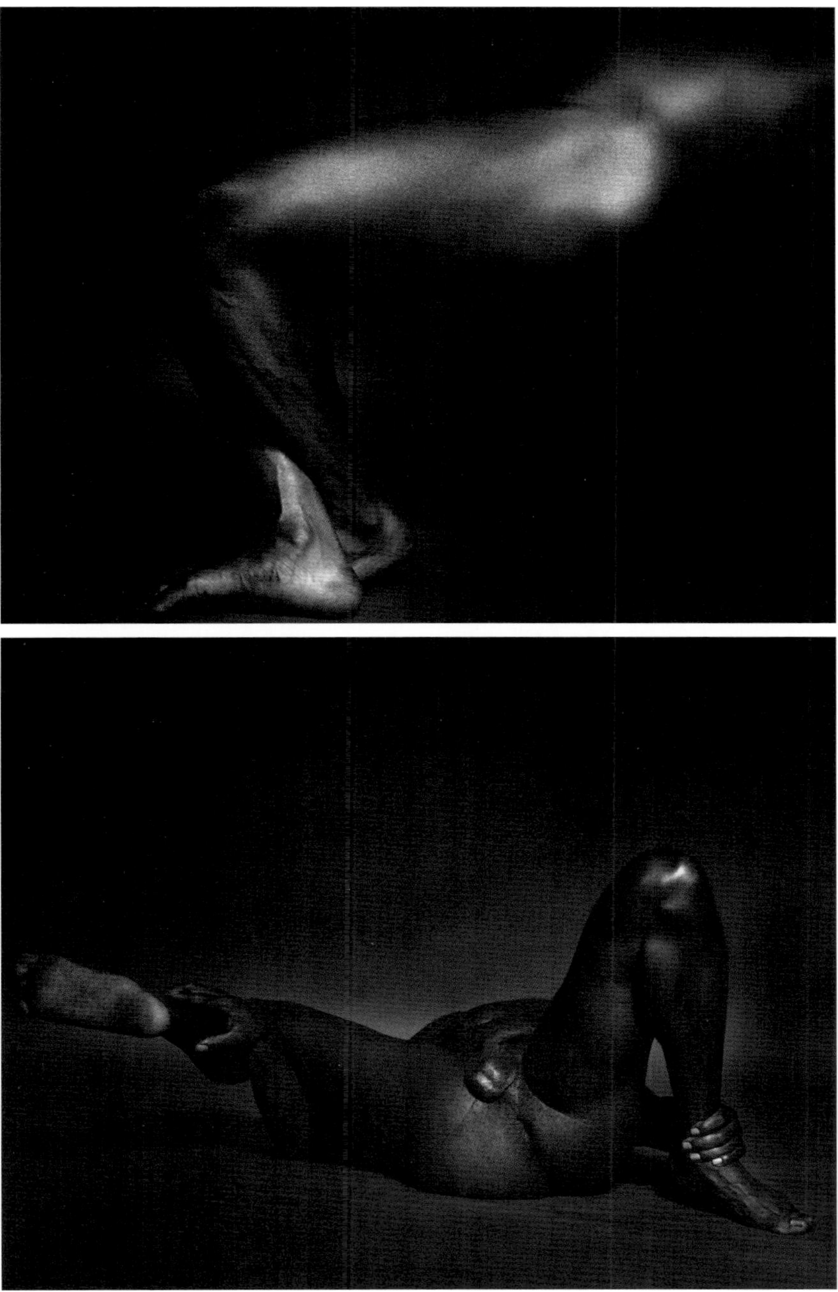

 PN 1916/63 - 8 2022, from the series Very Private

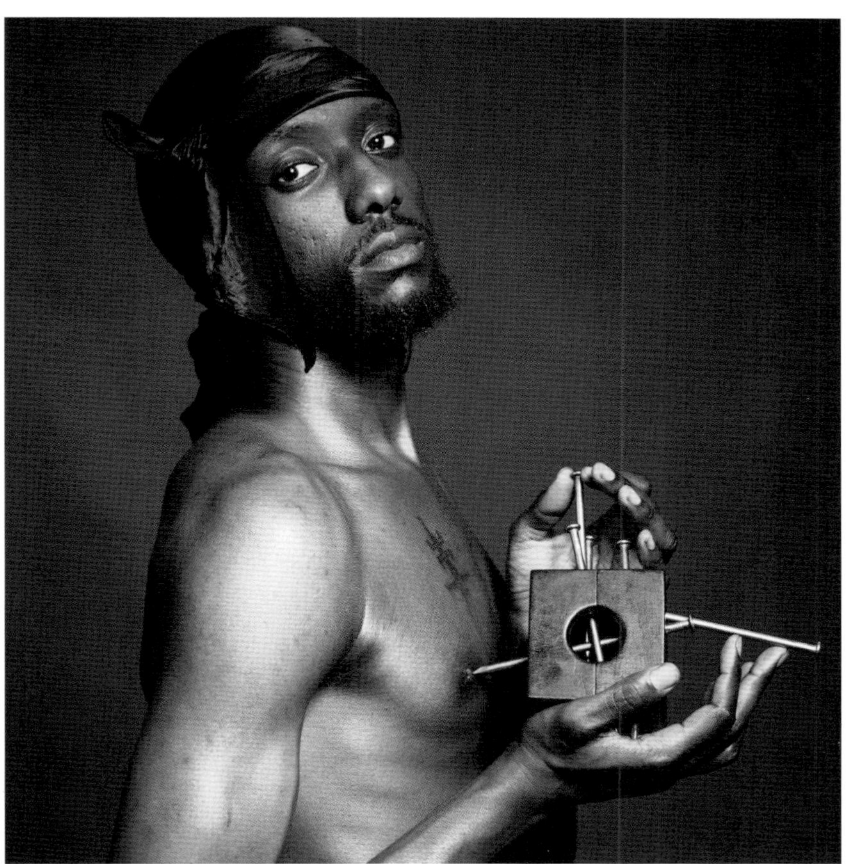

   Becoming Object 2022

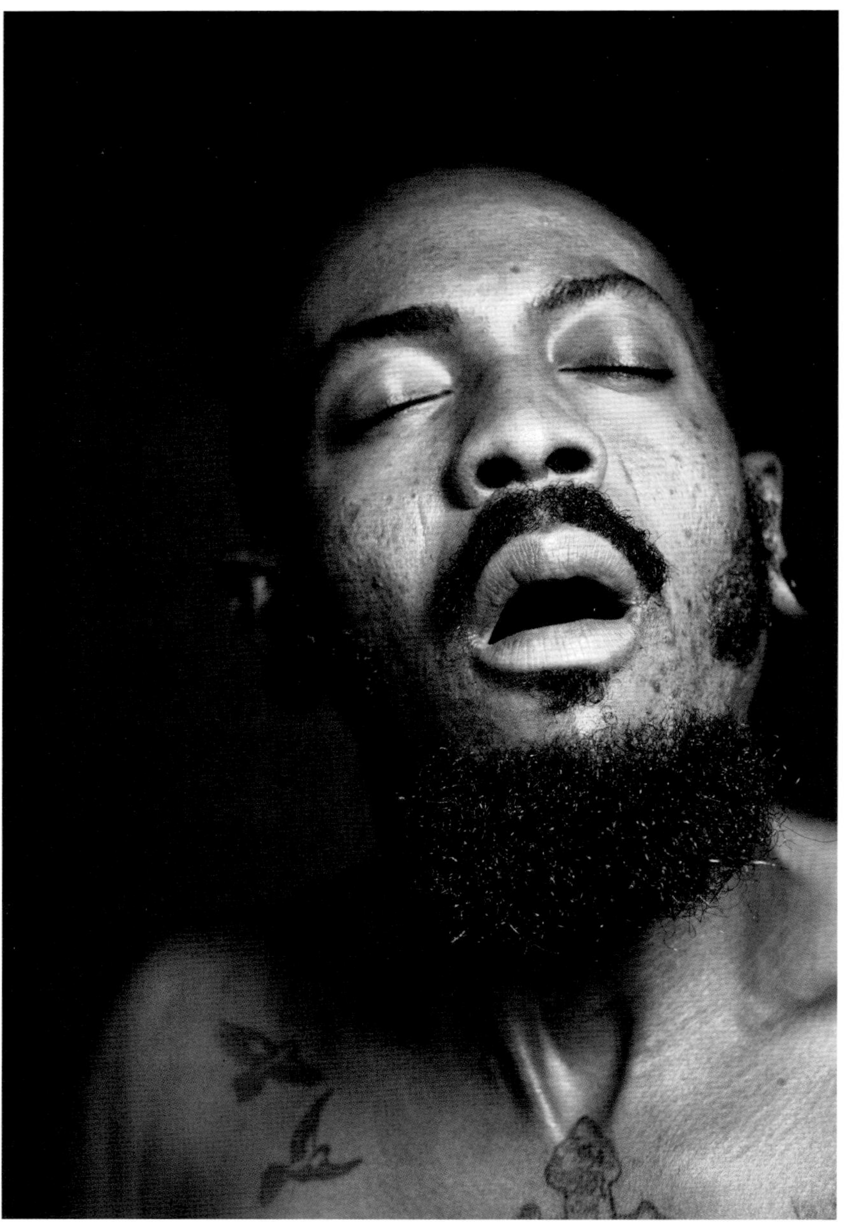

   Tattoboiadex 2022, from the Reluctant Voyeurs series

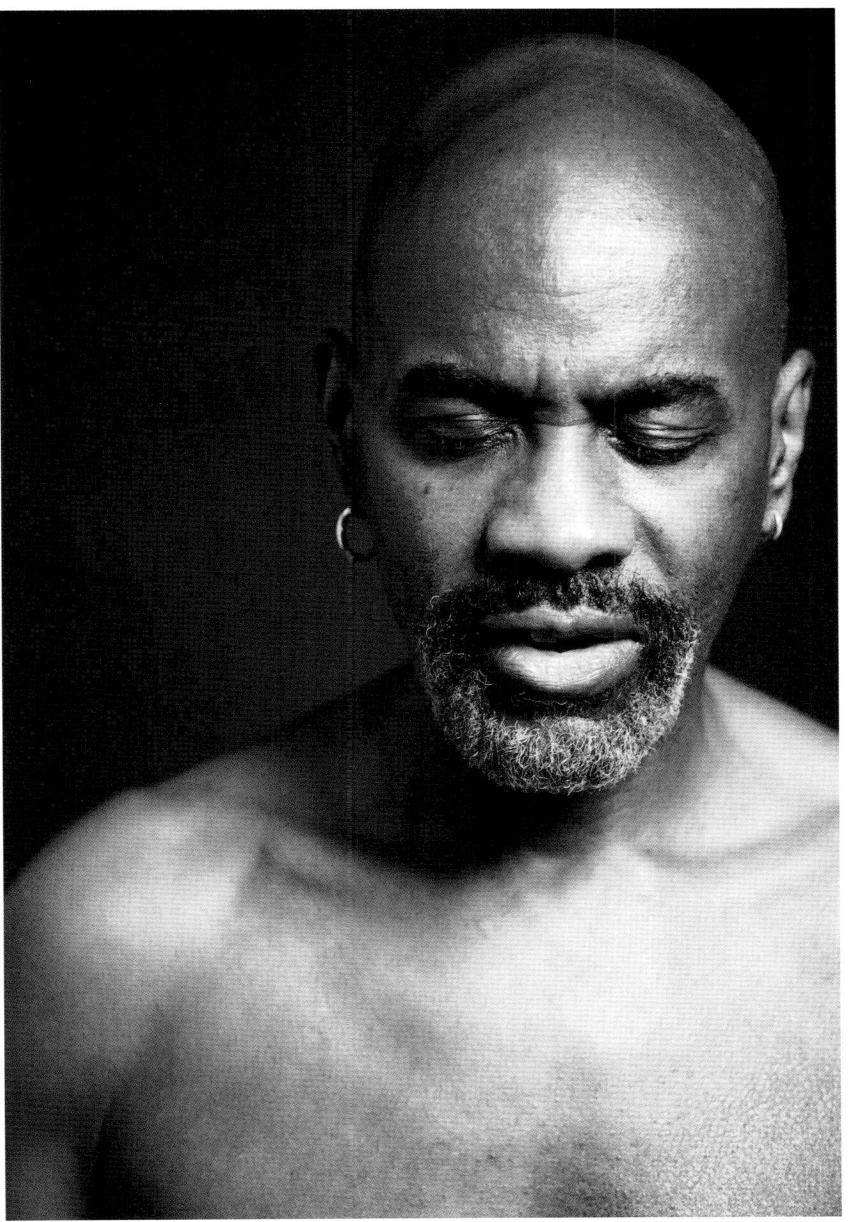

   Heverton 2022, from the Reluctant Voyeurs series

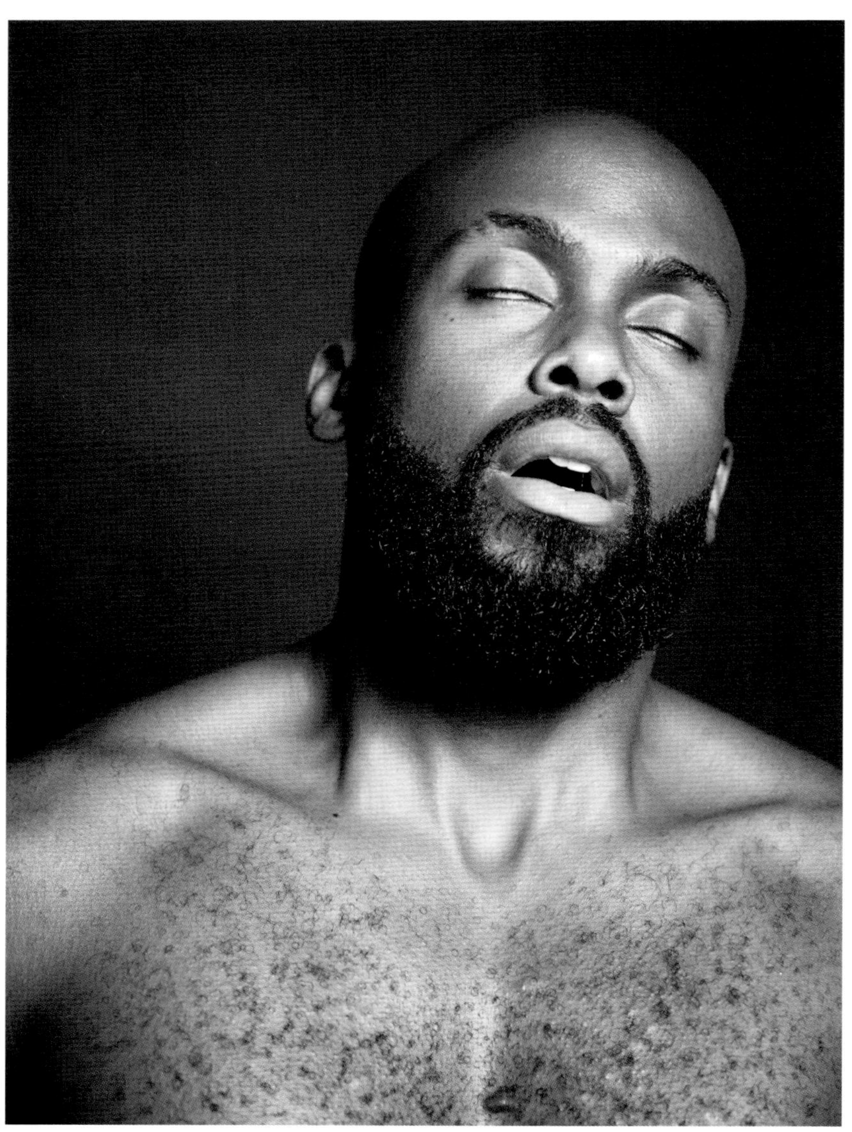

   Dwayne 2022, from the Reluctant Voyeurs series

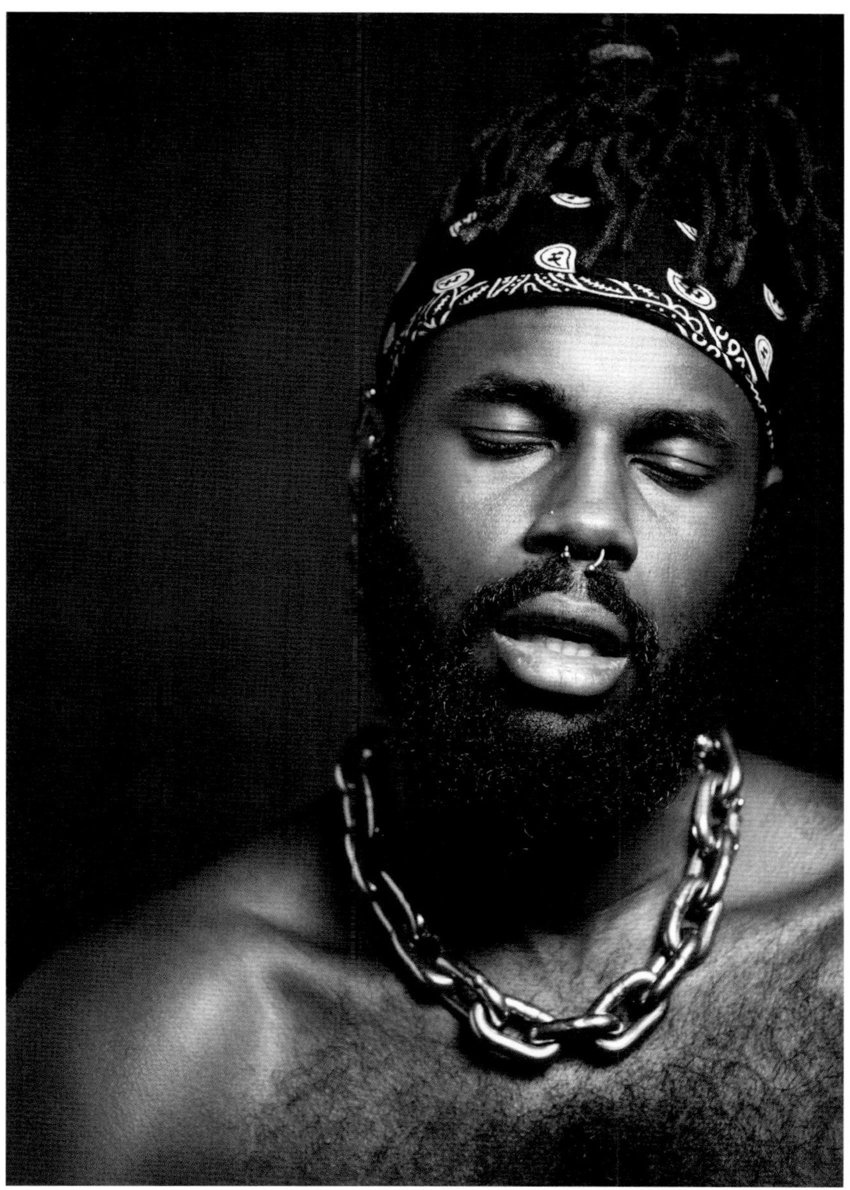

 Blaize 2022, from the Reluctant Voyeurs series

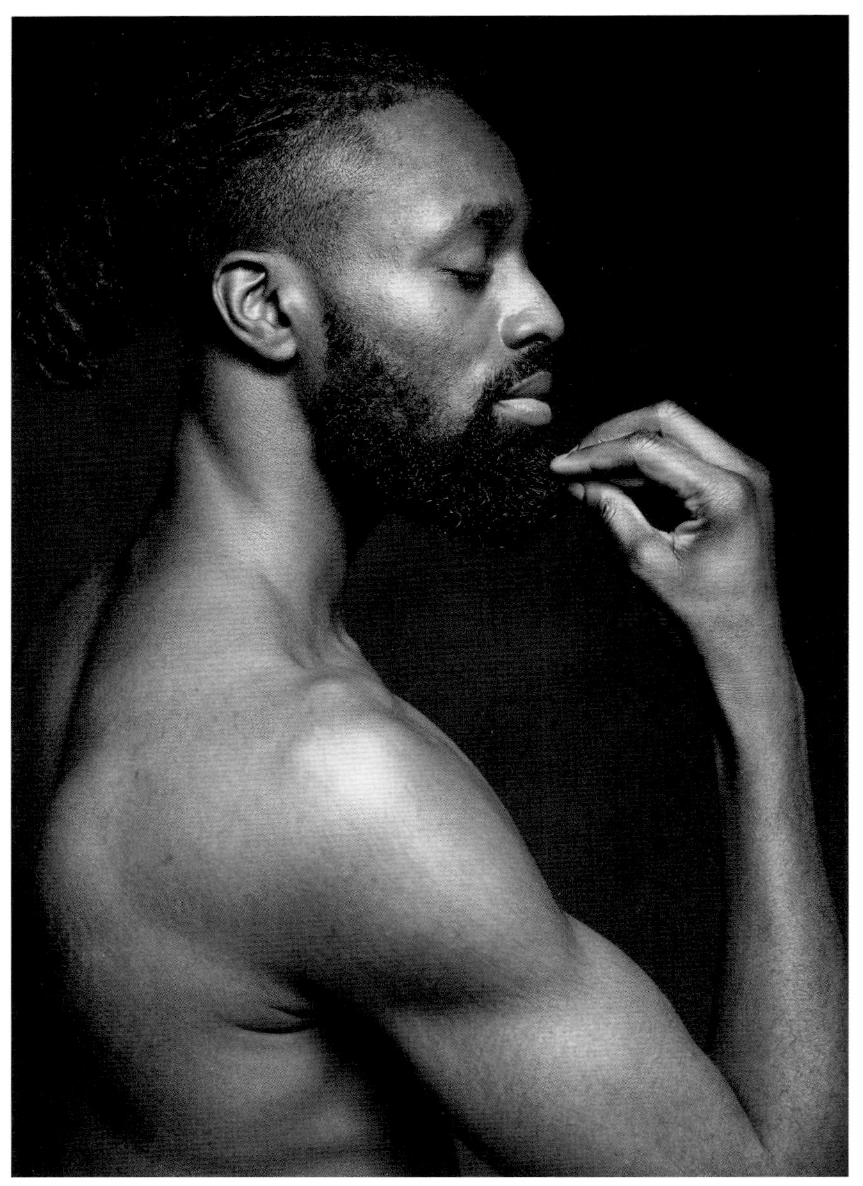

   Beard 2023

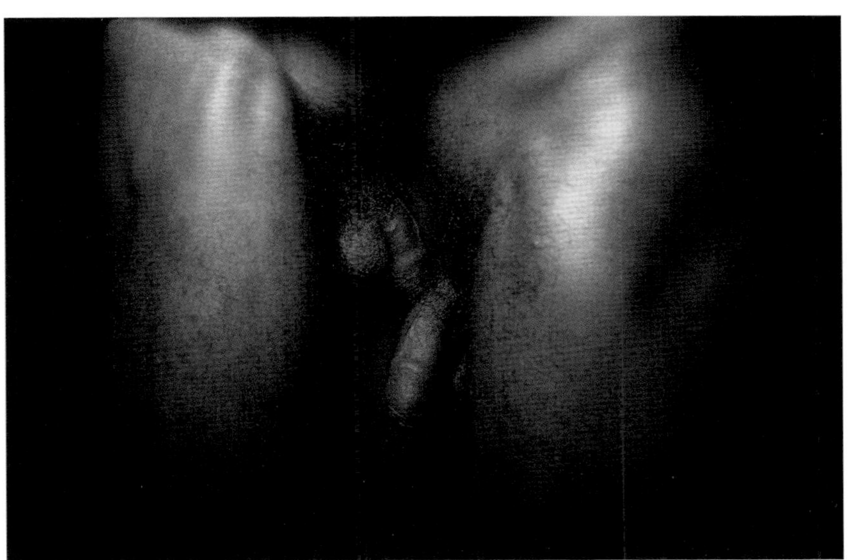

J and D 2023

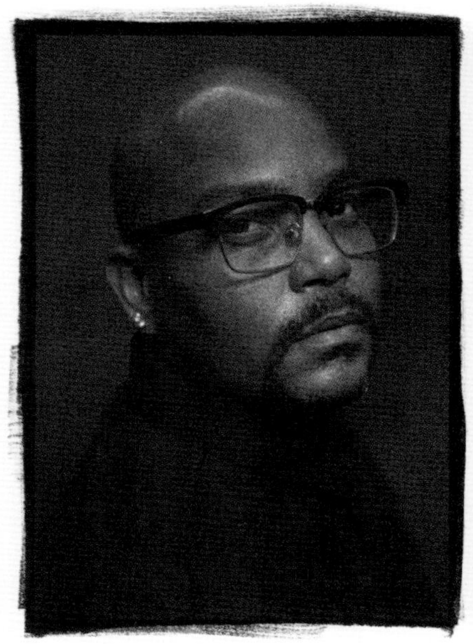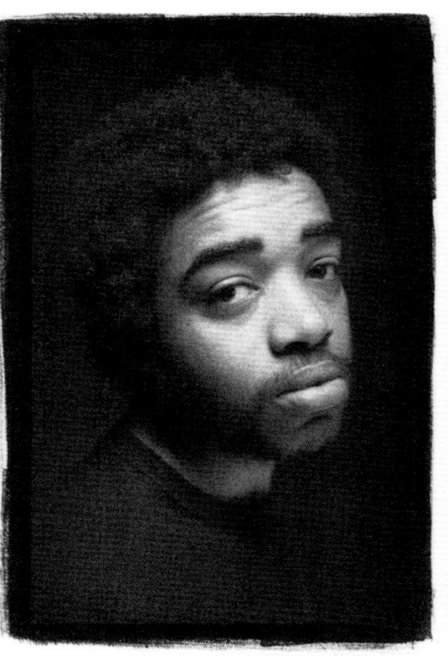

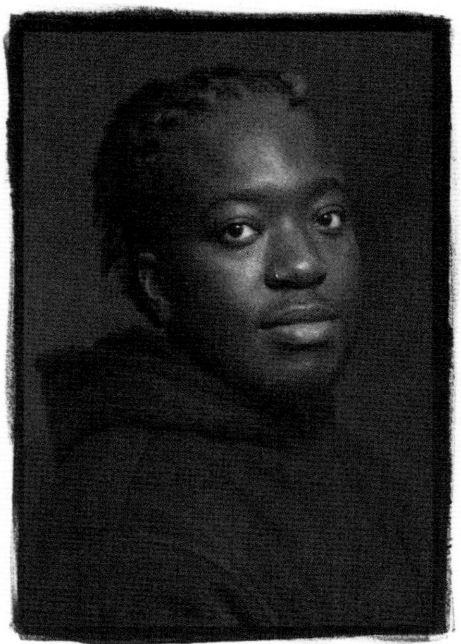

Chaune King 2023, from the Ecce Homo series
Albel Holsborough 2023, from the Ecce Homo series
Mels Owusu 2023, from the Ecce Homo series

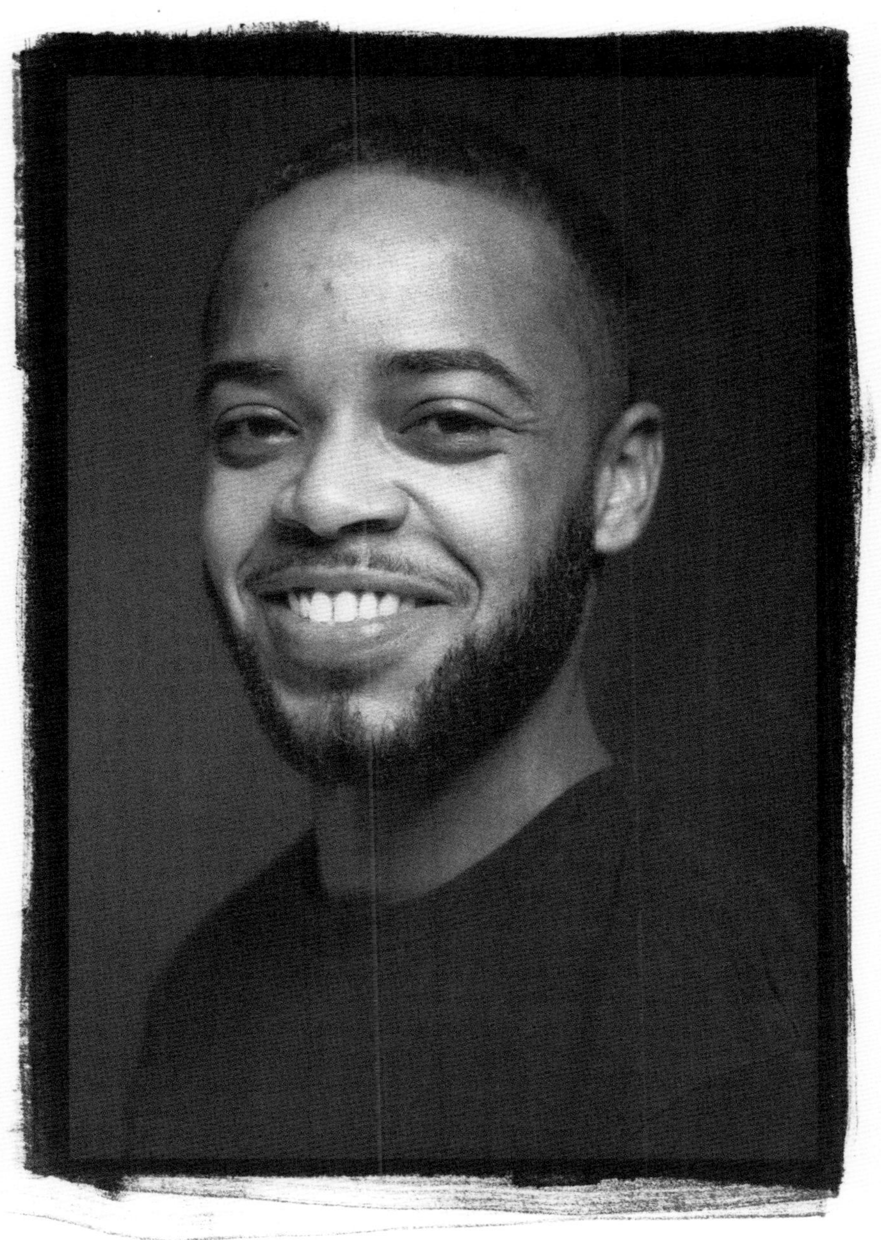

 Cole Daniel 2023, from the Ecce Homo series

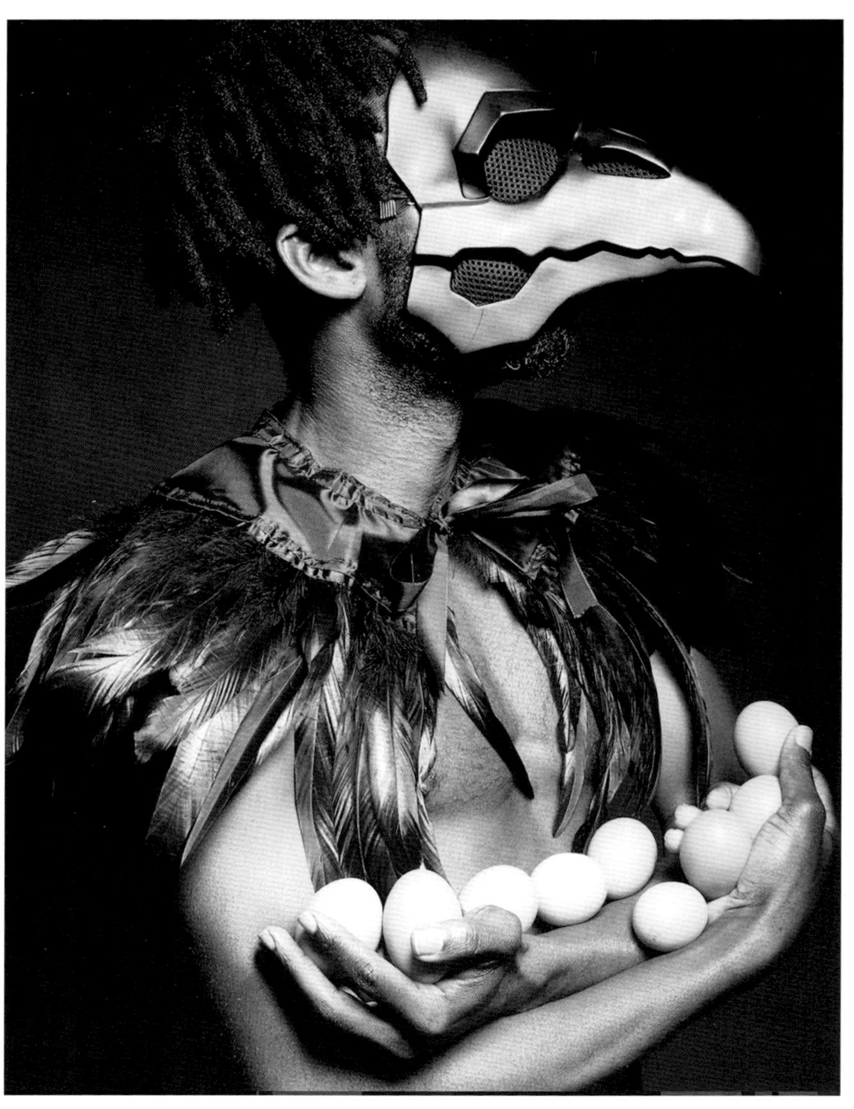

   Crow Bird Boy 2023

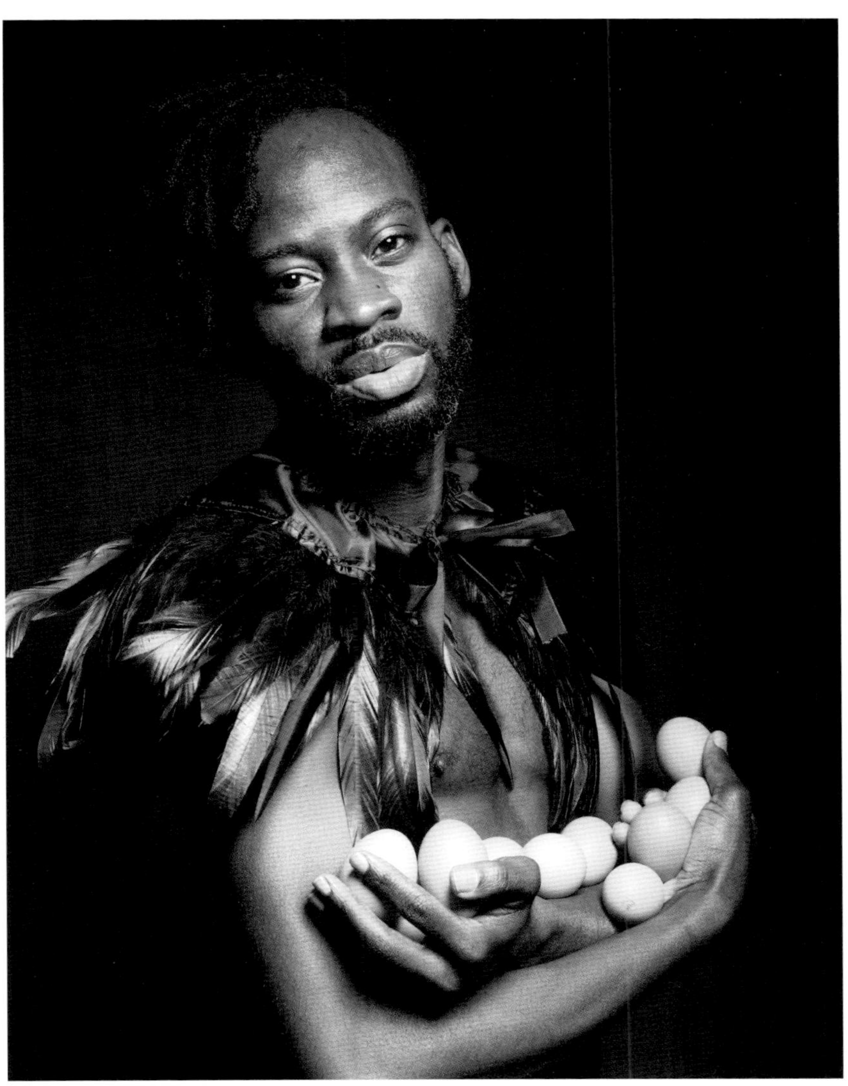

 Crow Bird Boy (unmasked) 2023

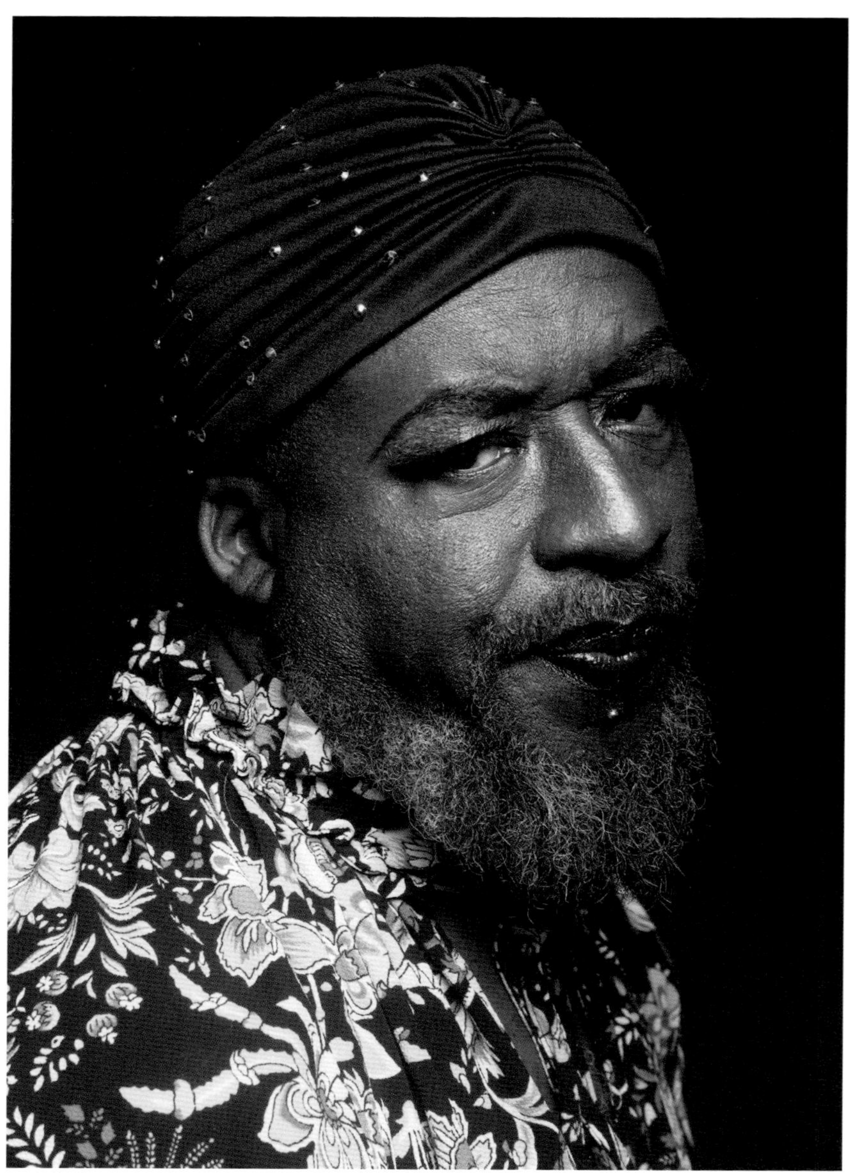

      Mz Mavis, Agony Artist 2023

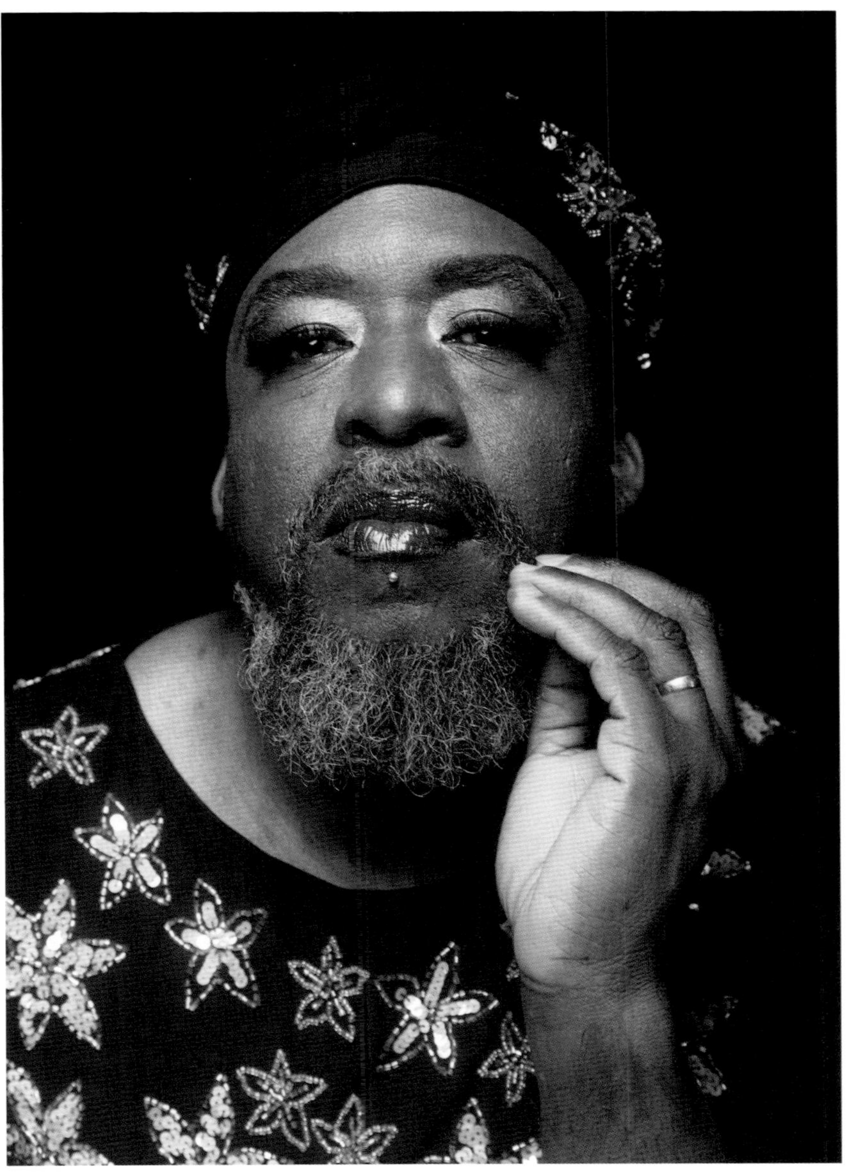

     Mz Mavis, Agony Artist 2024

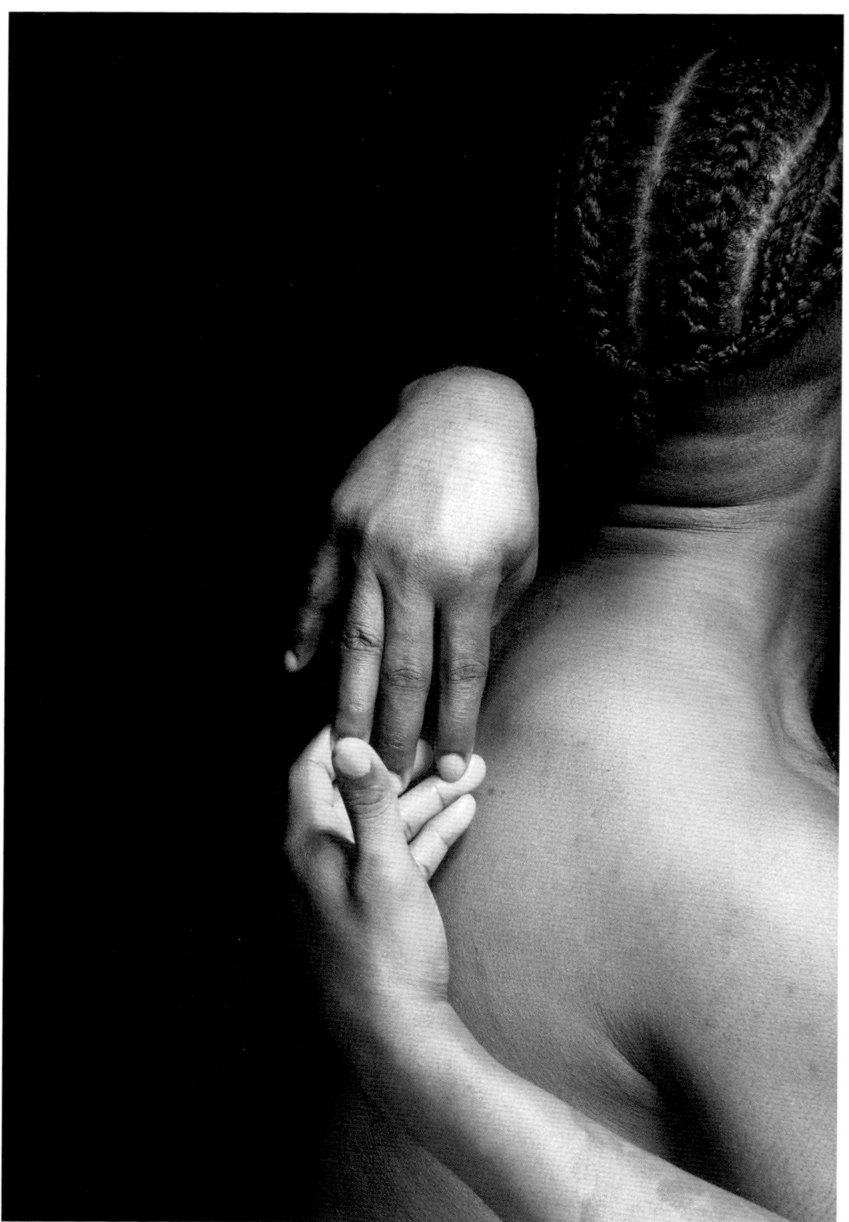

   From A Sensual Chorus of Gestures, 2024

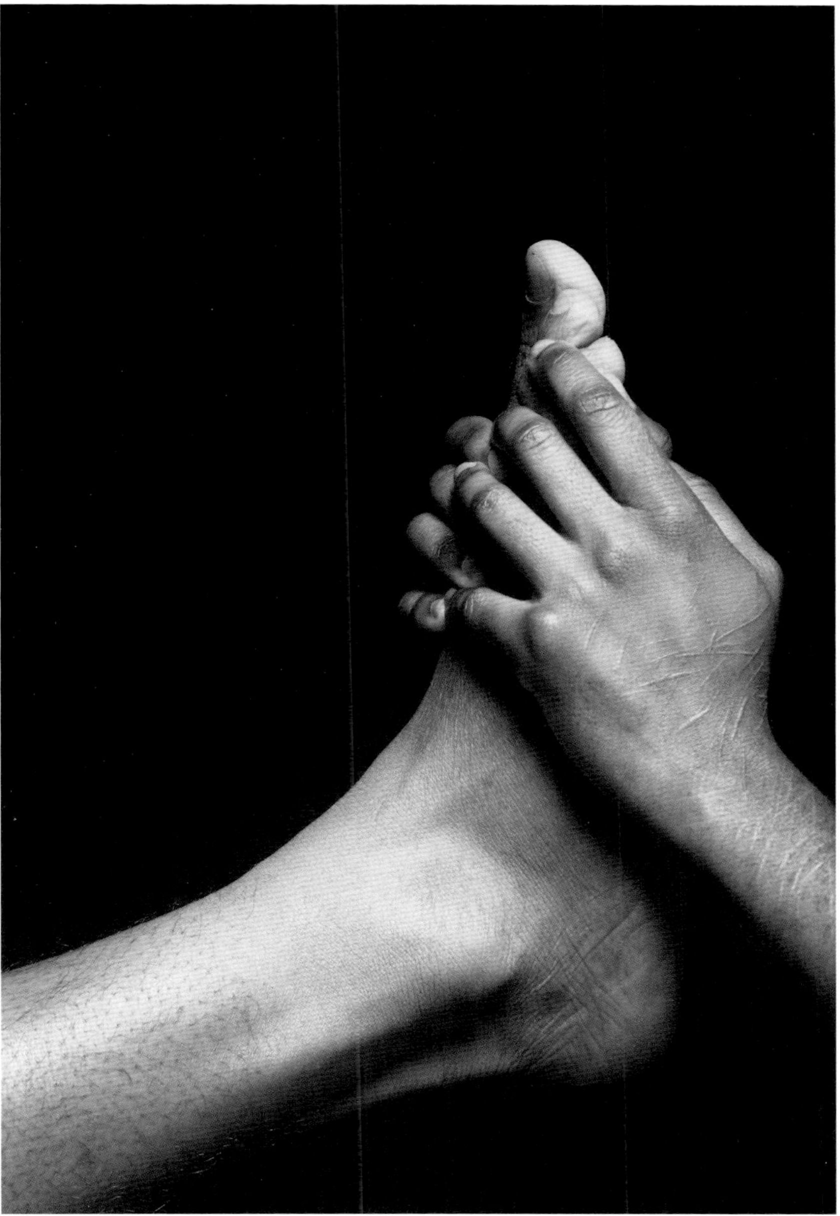

     From A Sensual Chorus of Gestures, 2024

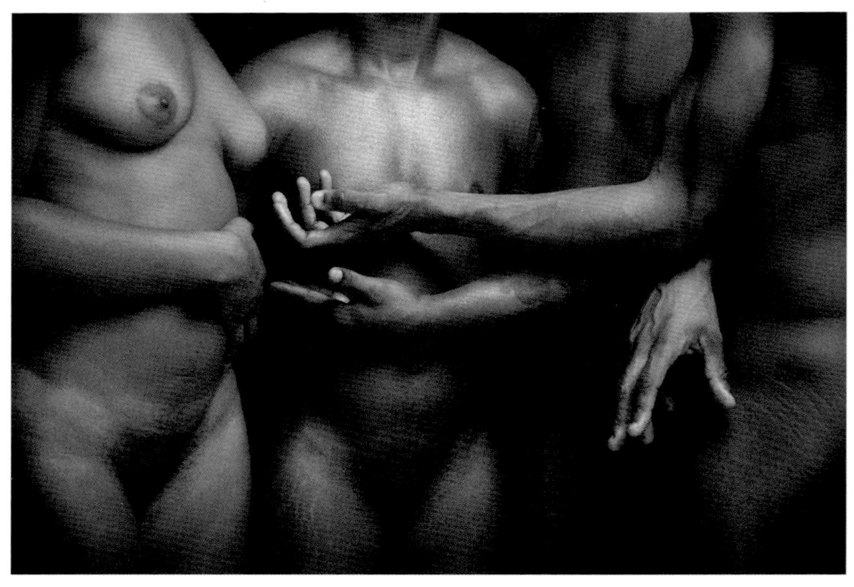

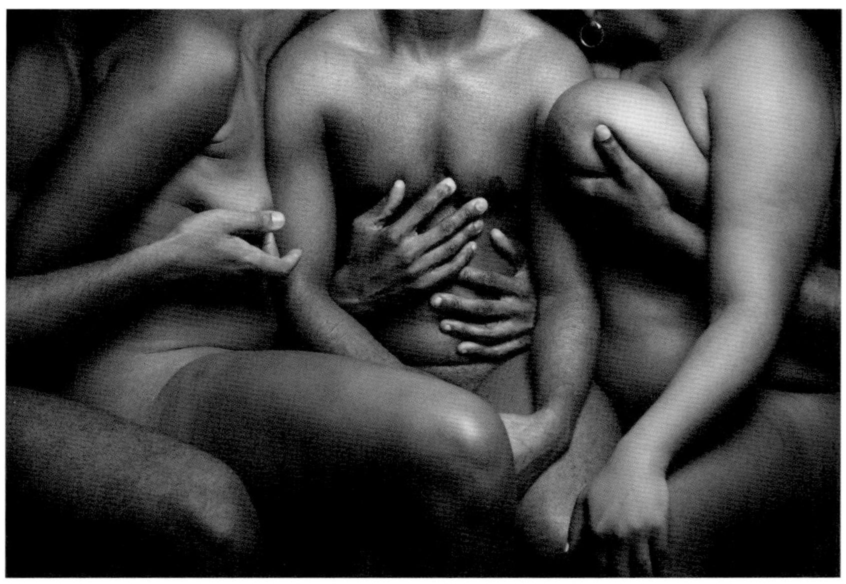

   From A Sensual Chorus of Gestures, 2024

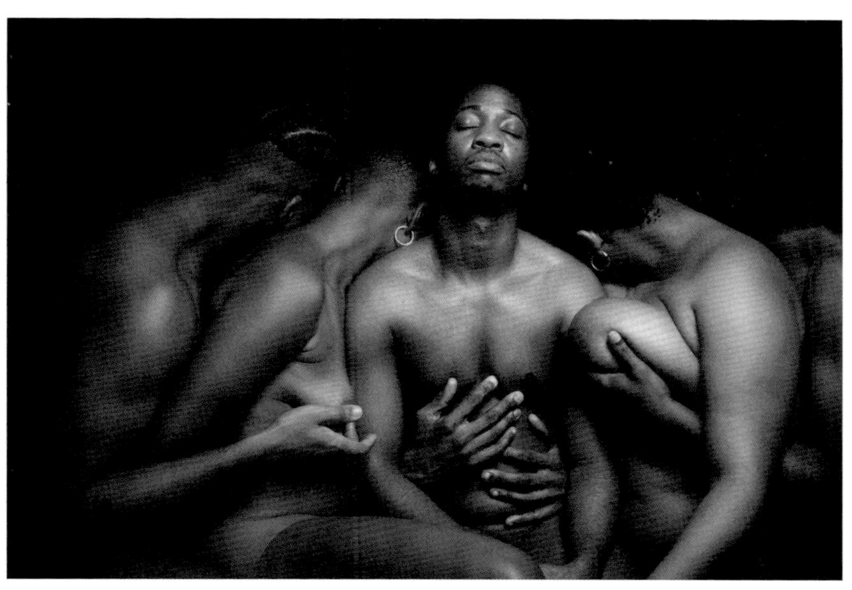

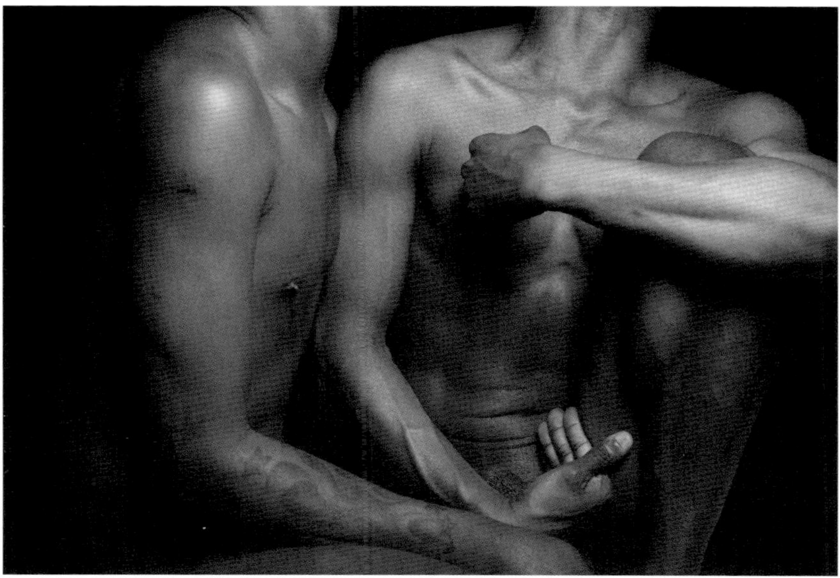

    From A Sensual Chorus of Gestures, 2024

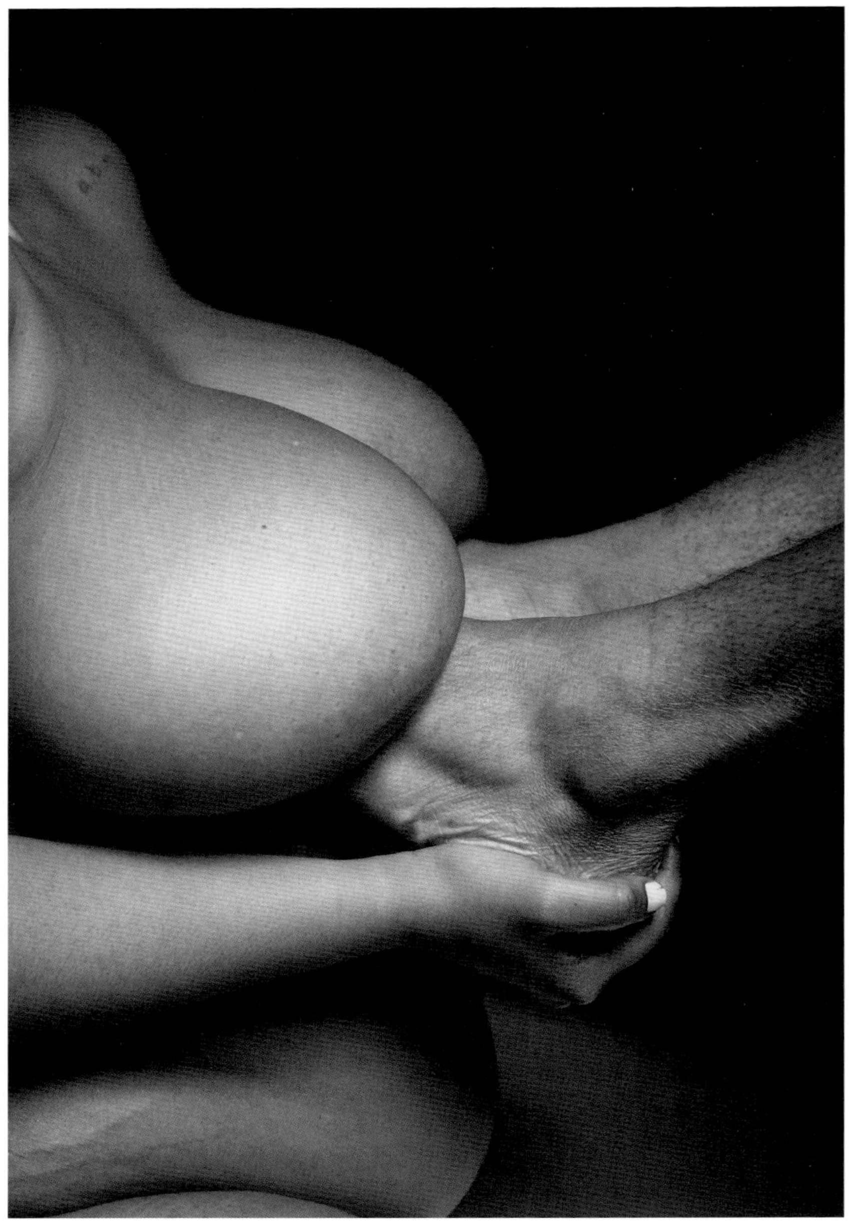

    From A Sensual Chorus of Gestures, 2024

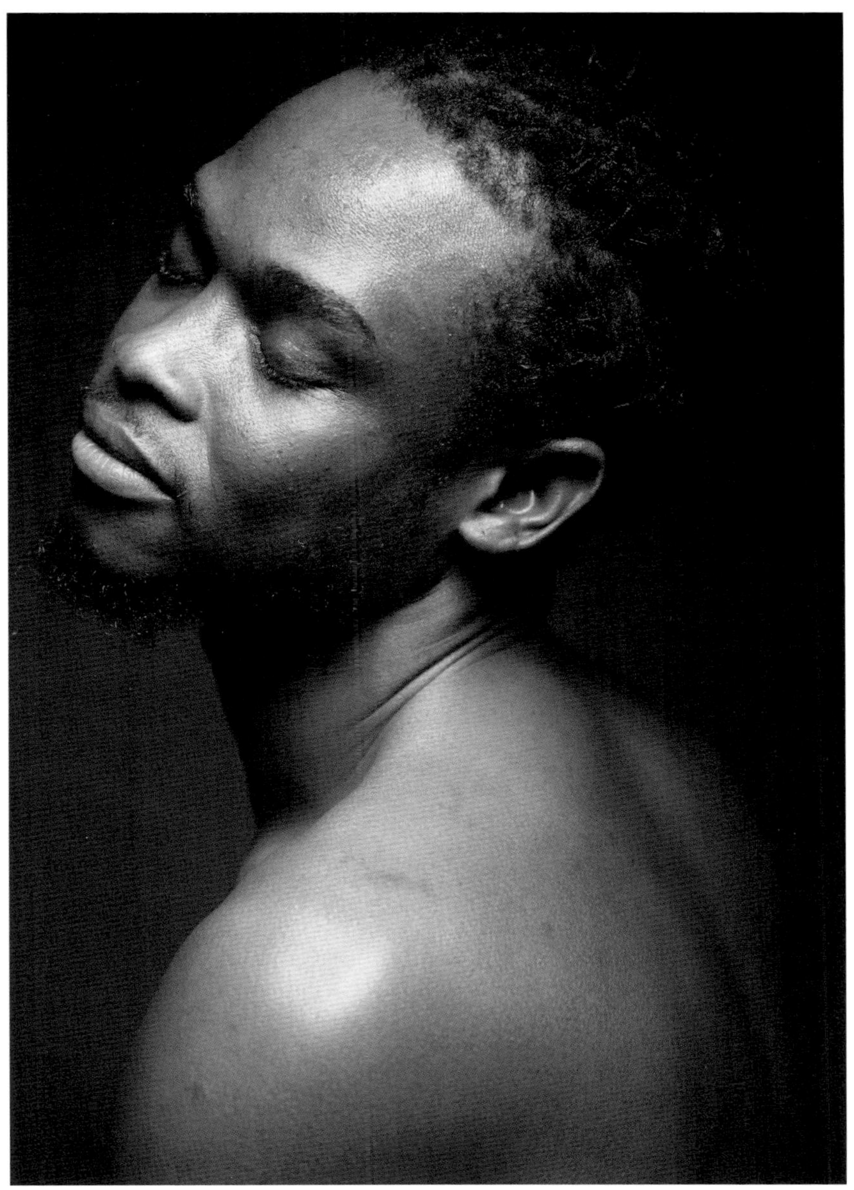

    Enitan 2024

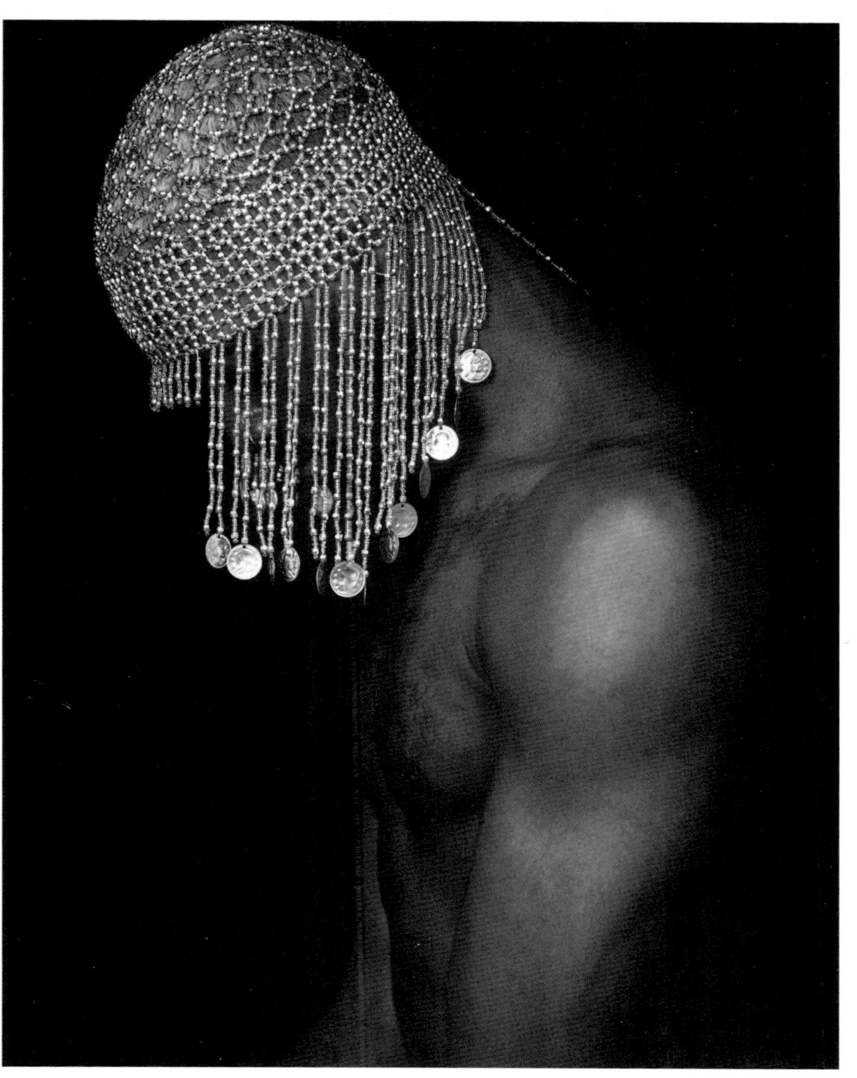

    Yusuf 2024

CREDITS

COPYRIGHT
All images © Ajamu X. All rights reserved, DACS, 2025

PHOTO CREDITS
All images courtesy the artist except where stated
otherwise
Pages 16–17 Photo: Tate

ARTIST'S ACKNOWLEDGEMENTS

To Friends, (ex) Lovers, Play Buddies and Muses (you
know who you are).